Why Bad Beats Good

Stop Your Brain's Negative Pull and Transform Your Relationships, Decisions, and Self-Worth

Simon Blackwood

First edition, 2026

Published by Simon Blackwood

Contents

Foreword

I did not set out to write about the negativity bias because it was the most elegant finding in the literature. I chose it because it is the one that costs people the most, quietly, in decisions they never think to reopen.

Every book in this series picks apart one well-documented distortion in how the mind weighs evidence. This one earned the earliest slot in the sequence because, of all of them, it is the hardest to catch in the act. Confirmation bias announces itself, eventually, when the contrary evidence finally piles up too high to ignore. The negativity bias does not announce itself at all. It simply arrives first, feels more important than it is, and leaves before anyone thinks to ask whether it earned the weight it was given. A hiring manager does not experience herself as overweighting two minutes out of forty. She experiences herself as remembering the interview accurately. That is what makes this particular distortion worth an entire book rather than a paragraph inside a larger one: it does not feel like a bias from the inside. It feels like judgment.

The personal stake, if a forensic-nonfiction writer is permitted one, is ordinary rather than dramatic. I have sat in enough conference rooms, read enough consumer reviews, and watched enough close elections to have noticed the pattern operating on my own judgment before I had a name for it — a single sharp criticism outlasting a week of quiet competence, a single bad headline outlasting a decade of slow improvement. Naming it did not make it stop. It made it visible enough to check.

This book does not ask a reader to feel less alarmed by bad news, a harsh review, or a disclosed risk. The research cited throughout suggests that alarm is not optional; it is largely automatic, inherited from an environment where it did real work keeping people alive. What the book offers instead is narrower: seven rooms in which the same asymmetry does measurable damage, and a closing chapter of techniques that intervene not in the feeling but in the verdict the feeling gets translated into. That gap — between an amplification nobody can switch off and a judgment that can still be audited — is where the whole book lives.

— Simon Blackwood

Introduction

Negativity bias isn't just a quirk of how you remember a performance review or choose a rice cooker online. It's an active force that erases good information in the presence of bad—and the higher the stakes, the more complete the erasure. This book is about what survives that filter, what doesn't, and what it costs us when one infection kills a program that saved thousands, when three minutes of testimony outweighs a week, when a stock that lost a million customers gets celebrated. The asymmetry is real. The question is whether we can measure our way past it.

Negativity bias isn't one thing going wrong in your head. It's a cascade. Bad information captures your attention first. Then it sticks in memory five times longer than good. Then gatekeepers select for it. Then you need five positive experiences to outweigh one negative just to stay level. Then rare risks dominate frequent benefits in high-stakes decisions. Then negative information placed last carries disproportionate weight. Then someone who understands all of this weaponizes it. Each mechanism compounds the last, from the personal to the institutional to the political, which is why knowing you're biased doesn't fix it.

This book examines one mechanism — the negativity bias — as it operates in seven unrelated settings: a performance review, a newsroom, a marriage, a trading floor, a doctor's office, a jury room, and a campaign war room. Chapter 1 defines the bias itself and traces its likely origin. Chapters 2 through 8 each plant that same bias in one domain and reconstruct, forensically, what was known, what was assumed, and what the distortion cost. Chapter 9 turns from diagnosis to defense.

The chapters can be read in order, which is how the book is built to work — each domain borrows a little from the one before it, and the techniques in the final chapter draw directly on findings established earlier. They can also be read out of order by a reader chasing one specific room: the workplace chapter and the relationships chapter stand on their own well enough for that.

Each chapter follows the same forensic shape. It opens on a concrete scene, moves into the research documenting the pattern in that domain, and closes with a short, second-person turn — headed "What this means for you" in every chapter but the first — that asks the reader to apply the chapter's finding to their own next decision rather than treat it as a case study about someone else. This is the only place in the book where the address turns direct; the rest stays in the analytical, third-person register the subject calls for.

A note on the case studies: every illustrative person in this book — the hiring manager, the marketing manager, the newspaper editor, the couple, the investor, the patient, the juror, the strategist — is an explicitly labeled composite, built from a pattern documented across real research rather than drawn from any single identifiable individual. Every named study, researcher, and historical incident, by contrast, is real, and is attributed in the Notes & Further Reading section at the back of this book. The two categories are never blurred in the text itself, and they should not be blurred by the reader either: the composites illustrate a documented pattern; the citations are what document it.

Nothing in this book asks the negativity bias to be switched off. It asks only that it be named, chapter by chapter, in a different room each time, until naming it becomes a habit that outlasts the book.

Chapter 1: The Weight of One Bad Word

I was shopping for a rice cooker last month—nothing fancy, just something to replace the one I'd broken—and I found myself doing exactly what I'm about to describe. Which is how I know this isn't something that happens to other people while we watch from a safe distance.

The listing I'd landed on had 237 reviews. I read maybe four of the five-stars, skimming mostly, the way you skim anything that confirms you're about to make a reasonable decision. Then I hit a one-star from someone whose cooker had arrived with a dent in the lid. She'd posted a photo. The dent was maybe the size of a dime.

The listing I'd landed on had 237 reviews. I read maybe four of the five-stars, skimming mostly, the way you skim anything that confirms you're about to make a reasonable decision. Then I hit a one-star from someone whose cooker had arrived with a dent in the lid. She'd posted a photo. The dent was maybe the size of a dime.

I read that review three times.

I checked the date—February 14th, recent enough to matter. I scrolled down looking for other reviews mentioning dents, or shipping damage, or quality control. I found two more one-stars—one about a smell the first time the cooker was used (which, for the record, literally every rice cooker I've ever owned has had), one about the timer being "unreliable," though the reviewer never said what that actually meant.

By the time I closed the tab, undecided, those three reviews had outweighed the other 234 combined. I didn't buy the cooker. I can't tell you now what a single one of the positive reviews actually said. I can still describe the dent.

This is not a story about being careful. It's a story about the way our minds weigh evidence when that evidence splits between good and bad. My mind—and yours, and the mind of every person who has ever scrolled through a set of reviews looking for the thing that will make the decision for them—doesn't weigh that evidence the way a spreadsheet would. A spreadsheet averages. It treats each review as one data point among many, adds them up, divides by the total, outputs a number.

We do something different. We find the bad ones first, work them over hardest, remember them longest, and then act as though the bad ones carry more truth than the good ones—even when the math says they don't.

Give this pattern a name and it turns out to be one of the oldest, most thoroughly documented findings in the study of how people make judgments: the negativity bias. Negative information—a fact, an event, a piece of feedback—gets weighted more heavily in our minds than positive information of equal size. Not more heavily because the negative information is objectively more important. More heavily because it's negative.

The mind's scale isn't balanced to begin with. It has a thumb already pressing down on one side before either piece of evidence lands on it.

That thumb is the subject of this book.

The asymmetry shows up everywhere, once you know to look for it. And it shows up precisely—not as vague folk wisdom about "bad news traveling fast" but as a measured, repeatable difference in how the brain processes information depending on whether that information registers as good or bad.

Take what happened to Susan Boyle in 2009. You might remember the moment. She walked onto the *Britain's Got Talent* stage—a forty-seven-year-old woman from a small Scottish village, unemployed, never been kissed (she said this on camera), dressed in a way that made the audience smirk before she'd sung a note. The cameras caught it. People rolling their eyes. One man shaking his head. Simon Cowell looking down at his notes with an expression that said he'd already made up his mind.

Then she opened her mouth and sang "I Dreamed a Dream" from *Les Misérables*, and the entire room went silent. Then they stood. The video of that audition has been watched hundreds of millions of times. It became one of the defining moments of reality television—the reminder that we shouldn't judge by appearances, that talent can come from anywhere, that cynicism sometimes gets it spectacularly wrong.

Here's what interests me about that moment: the thirty seconds before she sang.

Those thirty seconds—the smirks, the eye rolls, the visible dismissiveness from the judges and the audience—got processed and encoded into memory with a different weight than the three minutes of her actual performance. The negative snap judgment landed first, sank in deep, and then had to be *overcome* by her singing. The performance had to be extraordinary—not just good, but overwhelming—to budge that initial impression.

And here's the part that maps onto what we're talking about: if she'd walked out looking polished and confident, and then sung the exact same song with the exact same skill, the moment wouldn't have had anywhere near the same impact. The power of the performance came from the distance it had to travel to reverse the negative judgment the audience had already made in the first thirty seconds. The negativity bias created the hole. Her talent filled it. But the hole had to be dug first before the filling could register as remarkable.

Watch the video again if you haven't seen it in a while. Watch the faces in the audience during those first thirty seconds. That's not polite skepticism. That's contempt. Pre-loaded. Arrived at in the time it takes to register: middle-aged woman, unfashionable dress, frizzy hair, Scottish accent. Decision made. She hasn't opened her mouth yet and they've already written her off.

That's the weight of one bad word—or in this case, one bad first impression—before a single note of actual evidence arrives.

We saw this pattern play out again—darker, higher stakes—in the lead-up to the 2008 financial crisis. Plenty of people were sounding alarms. Plenty of data suggested the housing market was overvalued, that mortgage-backed securities were riskier than their ratings suggested, that leverage ratios at major banks had entered dangerous territory. But those warnings had to compete against years of positive news: rising home values, steady returns, a broad consensus among very smart, very credentialed people that the models were sound and the risks were managed.

The negative information—the warnings, the data showing cracks—should have been weighted heavily. It was specific. It was early. It was coming from people who'd done the math. But it wasn't, because it had to overcome an enormous pile of accumulated positive signals that had already shaped the consensus view. The positive information had sunk in first, anchored the baseline, and the negative information had to fight uphill against that anchor just to be taken seriously.

By the time the negative information finally outweighed the positive—by the time Lehman Brothers collapsed and the crisis became undeniable—the reversal was catastrophic. The same minds that had under-weighted negative signals for years suddenly swung the other direction and over-weighted them, pricing in worst-case scenarios across the entire market at once.

This is the whipsaw we're going to see again and again: we under-react to early negative signals when they contradict an established positive view, then we over-react to negative signals once the consensus has flipped and everyone is looking for confirmation that things are worse than we thought.

The asymmetry doesn't correct for context. It just applies the same formula in both directions, amplifying the negative whenever the negative is what we're primed to find.

Start with attention, because that's where the asymmetry begins—before we've even decided what to think about a piece of information, before we've consciously registered what it means.

Negative stimuli capture the eye faster than positive ones. Show someone a grid of faces—one angry face mixed among many neutral or happy ones—and they'll find the angry face faster than they'll find a single happy face planted among neutral or angry ones. The visual system scans for threats first and pleasant surprises second. The difference in reaction time is small enough to miss in any single instance and large enough to replicate reliably across thousands of trials.

This isn't something we decide to do. It happens before the decision.

I tested a version of this on myself last week—not in a lab, just scrolling through my phone. I opened Twitter (I know, I know) and tracked which tweets made me stop scrolling. The ones that stopped me weren't the positive ones, even when the positive ones were about topics I genuinely care about. A friend announcing good news: kept scrolling. A thoughtful thread about something I'd been thinking about: kept scrolling. Someone quote-tweeting someone else to call them an idiot: stopped. Read the whole thread. Felt vaguely worse about the world and didn't even notice until I'd already spent five minutes down that particular hole.

My attention didn't go where I wanted it to go. It went where the negativity bias sent it, which was toward the conflict, the criticism, the person being wrong in public.

This isn't unique to social media. It's just that social media makes the pattern visible in a way that's harder to ignore. The algorithm didn't make me stop on the negative tweet. The algorithm just learned, very quickly, that negative tweets make people stop, and then served more of them because that's what the data said we were paying attention to. The algorithm is amoral. It's optimizing for engagement. But engagement, it turns out, is asymmetrically triggered by negative information, so an amoral system optimizing for engagement will tilt negative by default—not because it wants to make us miserable, but because our own attention patterns have already voted for what gets amplified.

We built the algorithm. The algorithm learned from us. What it learned is that we pay more attention to bad news than good news, and now it's giving us what we already wanted, whether we wanted to want it or not.

Next, processing depth. Once a negative stimulus has captured attention, the mind does more work on it. The bad review gets reread. Dated. Cross-checked against the other reviews looking for a pattern. The good reviews get skimmed. This isn't laziness about the positive information—it's efficiency, in the sense that positive information, historically, rarely required urgent follow-up analysis. A pleasant surprise didn't usually need to be solved. A threat did.

Then memory.

Negative events are recalled more vividly, in more detail, and for longer than positive events of comparable size. Ask someone to describe the best compliment they received in the last year and the worst criticism, and the criticism will almost always come back sharper—more of the room remembered, more of the exact words, more of what the person was wearing.

I tested this on myself before I started writing this chapter. I asked myself to recall the best piece of feedback I'd gotten in the last twelve months and the worst. The best one took me a minute to even locate—it was from an editor I respect, something about a draft being "cleanly argued," and I remember feeling good about it at the time, but that's where the detail stops. The worst one I can play back like a recording. The person's exact phrasing. Where I was sitting when I read the email. The specific way my stomach dropped. The feedback itself wasn't even particularly harsh—it was a perfectly reasonable note about a section that hadn't landed—but my memory system treated it like breaking news and filed the compliment under "miscellaneous pleasant background noise."

This isn't because the criticism mattered more in any measurable, downstream sense. It's because the memory system treated it as though it did, at the moment of encoding, and that treatment is mostly irreversible after the fact.

Put attention, processing, and memory together and the result is what I experienced with that rice cooker listing: the negative gets found first, worked over hardest, remembered longest, so it exerts influence on the eventual judgment completely out of proportion to its actual share of the total evidence.

Think about what this means for something as ordinary as a performance review at work.

A manager sits down to write feedback for someone who's had a solid year. The employee met their goals. Shipped their projects on time. Collaborated well. There were a couple of moments where things didn't go as planned—a presentation that ran long and lost the room, a project handoff that got confused because the documentation wasn't clear.

The manager is a reasonable person. Fair. Not trying to be harsh. She opens a blank document and starts typing. The positive stuff comes out in generalities: "strong contributor," "met expectations," "good team player." She's not being vague on purpose. It's just that the good stuff blurs together in memory into a general sense of "this person does their job well," and there's no specific moment her mind keeps returning to as evidence.

Then she gets to the development areas—the part of the review where she's supposed to note what could improve—and suddenly the detail floods back. She remembers the presentation that ran long. She can see the moment the room started to drift. She remembers the exact Slack message where a teammate asked for clarification on the handoff documentation, and the mild frustration in the way the question was phrased. She writes a full paragraph about the presentation. Another paragraph about the documentation. She's not piling on. She's just writing what her memory is serving up in high resolution, which happens to be the negative stuff.

The employee gets the review and reads it the same way the manager's memory encoded it: the positive feedback barely registers, the critical feedback lands like a spotlight. "Strong contributor" gets skimmed. The paragraph about the presentation gets read three times, and each time it reads a little harsher, a little more like a warning that their job might be in jeopardy, even though nothing in the actual words says that.

Neither person is being unreasonable. Neither person is trying to distort the truth. They're both just running the same asymmetrical evaluative system, which means the negative moments—two moments out of an entire year—end up carrying more weight in both the writing and the reading than all the steady, solid work that made up the other 98% of the year.

Now multiply that dynamic across every performance review, every piece of feedback, every evaluation happening in every workplace. We wonder why people feel like their good work goes unnoticed. We wonder why employees leave jobs where they were, by any objective measure, performing well. Part of the answer is right here: the system that encodes performance and the system that recalls performance are both tilted toward the negative by default, so even when a manager is genuinely trying to be balanced, what gets encoded most vividly and recalled most readily is the critical feedback, and what shows up in the review—and what the employee takes away from the review—is a distorted picture that over-represents the mistakes and under-represents everything else.

This isn't a problem we can solve by telling managers to "be more positive." The managers aren't being negative on purpose. They're writing what their memory is giving them, and their memory is giving them an asymmetrical account of the year because that's what memory does with mixed evidence.

Here's where I need to stop and say something, because I can feel the objection forming and it's a reasonable one.

You might be thinking: "Okay, but isn't this negativity bias also the thing that keeps us safe? Isn't it good that we notice threats? Isn't the problem not that we have this bias but that we've lost real threats to worry about, so now we're just anxious about nothing?"

Yes and no.

Yes, the bias is adaptive in the narrow sense that it probably kept our ancestors alive in environments where missing a genuine threat could end your genetic line in a single afternoon. A mind even slightly tilted toward noticing and reacting to danger—at the cost of occasionally overreacting to harmless things or under-crediting real opportunities—will, on average, survive and reproduce more successfully than a mind that treats threats and opportunities as symmetrical inputs.

Natural selection doesn't require the threat-biased mind to be right more often. It only requires the threat-biased mind to be wrong less catastrophically. And the arithmetic of survival makes that a very different bar.

So yes, the bias is there for a reason. The wiring made sense in context.

But here's the no part, and this is what the rest of this book is about: the context has changed so dramatically that the wiring now misfires constantly, in ways that don't serve us at all.

An ancestral human, over an entire lifetime, might have encountered a genuinely life-threatening event—a real predator, a real famine, a real act of violence from a hostile group—a handful of times. Maybe a few dozen at the outer edge. Each of those encounters justified an enormous, whole-system reaction: flooding the body with stress hormones, seizing attention completely, laying down a memory sharp enough to prevent the same mistake twice.

That reaction now fires not a few dozen times across a lifetime but multiple times a day. Once for a curt reply to an email. Once for a drop in a stock price. Once for a single unkind comment on something posted online. Once for a headline about a danger that will never come near our actual lives.

The reaction itself hasn't scaled down to match the lower stakes of its modern triggers. It still shows up close to full strength, because the machinery has no dial for "important but not survival-important." It has one setting for negative information, tuned to a threat level the input rarely earns anymore.

We're walking around with a smoke detector calibrated for a house fire going off every time someone burns toast.

Let me show you what that actually costs, day to day, in ways you've almost certainly felt but maybe never traced back to the source.

You send a proposal to a client. Solid work—you spent two weeks on it, checked it three times, ran it past a colleague who knows the space. You send it off feeling pretty good. Three days later the client responds. The email is mostly positive. She likes the overall direction. She appreciates the level of detail. She has one concern about the timeline in section three—thinks it might be too aggressive given her team's current workload—and she wants to schedule a call to talk it through.

You read that email and your stomach tightens.

Not because the concern is unreasonable—it's not. Not because the project is in jeopardy—it isn't. But because your evaluative system has already found the one negative note in the response, pulled it out, held it up to the light, and made it the lens through which you now read the entire email.

The phrase "mostly positive" doesn't register as mostly positive. It registers as "positive except for the part that matters." The request to "schedule a call" doesn't land as a normal next step in a collaborative process. It lands as a warning sign that something is wrong, that you missed something, that the whole proposal might unravel once she starts asking questions.

You spend the rest of the afternoon replaying the timeline section in your head, looking for what you got wrong. You draft three different versions of a response email, each one more defensive than the last, before you delete them all and force yourself to wait until tomorrow to reply. The good parts of her feedback—the parts where she said she liked the direction, appreciated the detail—have already evaporated. You couldn't quote them back if someone asked.

That night, over dinner, someone asks how your day went. You say, "Fine, mostly. Client had some concerns about a proposal I sent."

You don't mention that the concerns were minor, or that most of the feedback was positive, because by now your memory of the email has compressed into a general sense of "the client wasn't happy," and that's the version that sticks.

The next morning you check your email first thing, hoping for a follow-up that will clarify the concern or soften it somehow. There's nothing. You spend the first hour of your workday mentally preparing for the call, running through explanations, anticipating objections, bracing for a conversation that—when it actually happens two days later—turns out to be straightforward, cordial, and resolved in fifteen minutes.

None of this was catastrophic. The project moved forward. The client relationship stayed intact. But you spent three days carrying a weight that the actual situation didn't justify. Three days of low-grade anxiety, of second-guessing your work, of bracing for a conflict that never materialized. And the kicker is that the client probably has no idea any of this happened. From her side, she sent balanced feedback, flagged one reasonable concern, got a professional response, hopped on a call, worked it out. Standard project stuff.

From your side, it felt like the whole thing was on the verge of falling apart.

That gap—between the size of the negative signal in reality and the size of it in your head—is the cost I'm talking about. It's not the kind of cost that shows up in a budget line or a performance metric. It's the cost of emotional energy spent on a threat that wasn't real. The cost of confidence eroded by a criticism that didn't actually undermine the work. The cost of relationships strained because we're reacting to the version of the feedback our negativity bias handed us, not the version the other person actually sent.

Now multiply that across a day. A week. A year. How many client emails have you over-processed? How many offhand comments from a manager or a partner or a friend have you replayed until they meant something darker than they did when they were first said? How many decisions have you second-guessed, opportunities have you walked away from, risks have you declined to take, because one piece of negative information—often a very small piece—outweighed a much larger body of evidence pointing the other way?

This is the weight we're carrying. And most of us have carried it so long we don't even notice it anymore. We think this is just what thinking feels like. Careful. Cautious. Realistic. We've rebranded the negativity bias as "being smart," as though the person who finds the problem first wins some kind of prize for clear-eyed realism.

But there's nothing clear-eyed about a system that consistently, measurably, predictably overweights one kind of information and underweights another. That's not realism. That's distortion. And the distortion has consequences.

Here's one of those consequences, and it's bigger than individual anxiety or second-guessing: we've professionalized this.

We've built entire industries around the production and distribution of negative information, and we've dressed it up as a social good. Journalism operates on the principle that bad news is more important than good news, because bad news signals a problem that needs solving and good news signals that things are fine and don't require intervention. Which would be reasonable if bad news and good news actually mapped onto important and unimportant in any reliable way. But they don't. They map onto negative and positive. And because of the negativity bias, we've let "negative" become a synonym for "important" without ever checking whether that synonymy is earned.

A plane crashes, killing 150 people, and it's front-page news for days. Thousands of planes land safely the same week and it doesn't make the news at all, because "plane lands safely" isn't news. Except that in terms of what we ought to know about the safety of air travel, the thousands of safe landings are vastly more informative than the single crash. The crash is an outlier. The safe landings are the pattern. But the crash gets the coverage, the analysis, the expert commentary, the multi-part investigative series, because it's negative, and negative captures attention, and attention is what the news is selling.

I'm not saying the crash shouldn't be covered. I'm saying the asymmetry in coverage creates an asymmetry in perception. If you only ever hear about the planes that crash and never hear about the planes that land safely, your mental model of how dangerous air travel is will be wildly miscalibrated. You'll overestimate the risk because your sample of evidence is biased toward the negative.

And here's the part that loops back to the individual psychology we started with: the news outlets aren't doing this because they're trying to mislead us. They're doing it because they're giving us what we've already demonstrated we'll pay attention to. The negativity bias is our bias. The media is just the amplifier.

Same thing happens in politics. A candidate can give a hundred speeches over the course of a campaign. Ninety-nine of them are fine—on-message, reasonable, well-delivered. One of them includes a gaffe, a slip of the tongue, a moment where they lose their train of thought and say something awkward. Which speech gets replayed? Which one do we remember? Which one becomes the thing everyone is talking about the next day?

The gaffe. Every time. Because the gaffe is negative, and negative gets weighted more heavily than positive, so the one bad moment ends up mattering more in the public's perception of the candidate than the ninety-nine competent moments that preceded it.

And then we wonder why politics feels so toxic, why every campaign turns into a race to find and amplify the other side's mistakes. We're not doing it because we're bad people. We're doing it because the negativity bias has made mistake-finding the most effective way to capture attention, and attention is how you win.

I could keep going. Medicine, where we spend enormous sums of money and attention on rare diseases and exotic risks while underinvesting in the boring, unsexy interventions—better diet, more exercise, basic preventive care—that would save far more lives. Parenting, where we've turned every potential danger into a national panic (kidnapping, tainted Halloween candy, predatory strangers at the playground) even as every measurable indicator of child safety has gotten better. Investing, where the fear of loss is so much stronger than the hope of gain that people routinely make decisions that leave them poorer in the long run just to avoid the psychological pain of a short-term drop.

The pattern is everywhere. We've taken a cognitive bias that made sense in small doses, in an environment where threats were rare and survival was fragile, and we've scaled it up into a civilizational-level filter through which all information now has to pass. And because the filter tilts negative, the world that reaches us through the filter looks more dangerous, more broken, more hostile than the world actually is.

Which brings us to the real cost.

The real cost isn't just that we're anxious, though we are. It's not just that we're misinformed, though we are. It's that we've stopped being able to hear good news even when it's true. Even when it's backed by evidence. Even when it's shouted at us by every credible source in the room.

Child mortality is down. Extreme poverty is down. Literacy is up. Life expectancy is up. Violence is down. These aren't opinions. These are measurements, taken over decades, replicated across countries, confirmed by every major international organization that tracks this stuff. The world has gotten measurably, dramatically better on nearly every indicator of human welfare we have data for.

And if you polled a hundred people on the street and asked them whether things are getting better or getting worse, the overwhelming majority would say worse.

That's the negativity bias at civilizational scale. We've weighted the bad news so heavily that it's drowned out the good news entirely. Not because the good news isn't real. Because the architecture of our attention, our processing, our memory, and our media has made it functionally invisible.

So what do we do about it?

And here's where I need to be careful, because the easy answer—the answer that shows up in a lot of self-help advice and positive-thinking books—is something like "just focus on the positive" or "choose gratitude" or "look for the good in every situation." And I'm going to tell you right now: that's not the answer. That's a band-aid on a broken scale. It doesn't fix the underlying asymmetry. It just asks you to work harder to notice the positive information that your brain is systematically underweighting, which is exhausting and, for most people, unsustainable.

The real answer starts with seeing the bias for what it is. Not a character flaw. Not a sign that you're pessimistic or broken or doing life wrong. A systematic distortion in the way evidence gets processed, the same way a bent lens produces a bent image regardless of what you're looking at.

Once you see it, you can start to correct for it. Not by forcing yourself to "think positive," but by asking a very specific question when you catch yourself weighting a piece of negative information heavily: *Is this weight proportional to the evidence?*

Let me make that concrete.

The next time you get feedback—from a manager, from a client, from a partner, from anyone whose opinion matters to you—and that feedback includes both positive and negative elements, do this:

Stop before you react. Literally pause. And then count.

How many pieces of positive feedback did you get? Write them down if you have to, because your memory isn't going to hold onto them the way it holds onto the criticism.

How many pieces of negative feedback did you get? Write those down too.

Now look at the ratio. If you got ten positive comments and one negative one, and your emotional reaction to the feedback is being driven primarily by the one negative comment, you're watching the negativity bias in action. The weight you're giving that one comment is not proportional to the evidence. It's proportional to the bias.

That doesn't mean the negative feedback doesn't matter. It might be important. It might be pointing at something real that you need to fix. But it doesn't matter *ten times as much* as each piece of positive feedback just because it's negative. The scale is lying to you. And once you see that it's lying, you can start to adjust.

You can say to yourself: "Okay. There's one thing here I need to work on. And there are ten things I'm doing well. Both of those statements are true. I'm going to spend proportional time thinking about each."

And then—this is the hard part—you actually have to spend time thinking about the positive feedback. Not skimming it. Not dismissing it as "nice but not useful." Actually processing it the way you would process the criticism. What specifically did they say they liked? Why did it work? What does that tell you about what to keep doing?

This feels unnatural at first, because the bias makes the negative information feel more important, more urgent, more real. But the unnaturalness is the tell. If it feels weird to give the positive feedback equal weight, that's a sign that the scale was bent to begin with.

You can do the same thing with news. If you find yourself reading five articles about things that are going wrong in the world and zero articles about things that are going right, stop and ask: is this ratio giving me an accurate picture of reality, or is it giving me a picture that's been distorted by the media's business model and my own attentional bias?

Then go find one piece of good news. Deliberately. A measurable improvement in something that matters. It's out there—you just have to look for it, because the algorithm isn't going to serve it to you.

You can do this with reviews before you buy something. If you're about to let three one-star reviews outweigh 234 five-star reviews, stop and ask: what would have to be true for those three reviews to be more informative than the other 234? Maybe the answer is that the three are more detailed, or more recent, or they're all pointing at the same specific problem. Okay, fine, weight them more heavily. But if the only reason you're weighting them more heavily is that they're negative, that's the bias, not the evidence.

And you can do this—I would argue you have to do this—with people. If you're in a relationship where you can recall every critical thing the other person has said to you in the last year but you can't recall the compliments, your mental record of that relationship is distorted. Maybe the relationship actually is bad and the criticism is warranted. Or maybe the negativity bias has handed you a version of the relationship that overrepresents the conflicts and underrepresents everything else, and you're about to make a decision based on that distorted version.

Count. Make yourself count. The scale won't correct itself.

The weight of one bad word is real. The negativity bias is not something you can think your way out of, because it operates below the level of conscious thought. It's wired in. It's going to keep finding the bad reviews first, processing them hardest, remembering them longest.

But what you can do—what this entire book is about—is learn to see when the bias is doing its work, and learn to ask whether the weight it's putting on that one bad word is the weight that word actually deserves.

Because here's what I've learned, both from the research and from watching this play out in my own life: the negativity bias doesn't just make us more anxious or more pessimistic. It makes us miscalibrated. We walk around with a model of the world that consistently, predictably overestimates how bad things are and underestimates how good they are. And then we make decisions—about jobs, about relationships, about risk, about what to pay attention to and what to ignore—based on that miscalibrated model.

And those decisions compound.

The employee who gets mostly positive feedback but can only remember the criticism leaves a job that was actually good for them because their mental record says the job was mostly criticism. The client who sends a proposal that gets mostly positive feedback but one reasonable concern spends three days in a state of low-grade panic because their mind turned "one concern" into "the whole thing is falling apart." The voter who hears one gaffe from a candidate and ninety-nine competent speeches votes based on the gaffe, because the gaffe is what stuck.

None of these people are being irrational. They're all responding to the evidence their minds served up. The problem is that their minds are serving up a distorted sample.

The work is learning to see the distortion. And then learning to correct for it, one decision at a time, one piece of feedback at a time, one proposal at a time, one rice cooker listing at a time.

It's not sexy work. It doesn't come with a dramatic before-and-after. You don't wake up one morning and find that the negativity bias has vanished and your mind now weighs evidence symmetrically.

But you do start to catch it. You start to notice when your stomach tightens at one critical comment in an otherwise positive email, and you stop and count, and you realize the tightness is out of proportion to the evidence. You start to notice when you're about to skip a purchase because of three bad reviews out of 237, and you stop and ask whether those three reviews actually tell you something the other 234 don't.

And over time—slowly, unglamorously—you start making better decisions. Not because you've become more optimistic. Because you've become more accurate.

That's the promise this chapter is making. Not that you'll feel better. Not that you'll "think positive." That you'll see the scale for what it is—bent, but bent in a predictable direction—and you'll learn to adjust your readings accordingly.

The rest of this book is about how.

The dent was the size of a dime. The review section was 237 approvals wide. The dent won.

The dent was the size of a dime. The review section was 237 approvals wide. The dent won. And somewhere, right now, you're doing the same math and getting the same answer.

Chapter 2: The One Comment You Remember

The words your boss used to compliment your presentation last month? Somewhere in there, probably. Something about good energy, clear slides, maybe a line about how the stakeholders seemed engaged.

Now: the words she used when she said the financial projections in slide twelve didn't match the summary on slide three?

Those you can quote.

Now: the words she used when she said the financial projections in slide twelve didn't match the summary on slide three?

Those you can quote.

Not just the gist. The exact phrasing. The pause before she said it. Whether she was looking at her laptop or at you. Possibly even what you were wearing, what the room smelled like, whether anyone else was on the call.

This isn't because you're neurotic or because your boss delivered the criticism poorly. It's because negative information gets written into memory with a different pen than positive information does. Deeper ink. More pressure. The kind that leaves an impression on the page underneath.

Teresa Amabile, a researcher at Harvard Business School, spent years tracking what people remember from their workdays. She asked hundreds of knowledge workers to keep daily diaries of events that stood out to them — wins, setbacks, feedback received, ideas that went somewhere or nowhere. Then she followed up weeks later to see what had stuck.

The pattern was clean enough to feel inevitable once you saw it: negative events came back sharp. People could reconstruct conversations, remember who said what, recall the exact moment they realized a project was going sideways. Positive events blurred into gist. “My manager said something nice about the report.” “The client seemed happy.” The detail was gone, and with it most of the emotional weight.

We don’t forget praise because we’re ungrateful. We forget it because our brains never encoded it with the same depth they used for the criticism.

Picture Kim Scott — the woman who wrote *Radical Candor* and spent years at Google and Apple building feedback cultures — sitting in her office at Google in 2004, trying to figure out why a management training program she’d designed kept producing the opposite of what she’d intended.

The training taught managers to deliver balanced feedback. Specificity on both sides. Clear examples of what was working and what wasn’t. A structure designed to prevent the thing everyone fears most in performance reviews: vague criticism that lands like a verdict with no path to appeal.

The managers went through the training. They delivered the feedback exactly as taught. Specific praise, specific criticism, roughly equal time on both.

And their direct reports walked out of the meetings remembering only the criticism.

Not because the managers had bungled the delivery. Not because the employees were fragile. But because the system — the performance review itself, the scheduled appointment, the closed-door room, the manager with formal authority sitting across the table — had activated a kind of threat-detection mode that turned the employees' attention into a heat-seeking missile for anything that sounded like danger.

You walk into a performance review already asking yourself what you did wrong. Already scanning for the but that's coming. Already braced for the one thing that's going to be the real reason you're sitting there, no matter how much positive preamble surrounds it.

When the criticism arrives — even mild, well-intentioned, proportionate criticism — your brain doesn't process it the way it would process the same words delivered over lunch. It processes it the way you process the sound of your name being shouted in a tone you've never heard your spouse use before. Full attention. Immediate prioritization. Everything else fades.

The eleven positive bullets become "she said it went well." The one negative bullet becomes the thing you lie awake thinking about at two in the morning, word for word, like you're preparing for trial.

Let me tell you what I did to my daughter.

Spring recital, age nine. She'd been nervous all week about one song she was performing from memory — a little Chopin prelude, maybe ninety seconds long, that she'd been drilling every night after dinner until I could hum it in my sleep.

She played it beautifully. Didn't miss a note.

She also played three other pieces that night. Two from the book, one that was a duet with her teacher. All of them went fine. One of the duets had a moment — maybe eight bars in the middle — where I could hear she'd rushed slightly and lost the tempo for a beat or two before catching up.

So at dinner afterward, I asked her about it.

Not in a mean way. Not even in a critical way, really. Just curious. Gentle. The way you ask a question when you're genuinely trying to understand what happened. *What was going on there? Did you lose your place? Were you rushing?*

She answered patiently at first. Then more quietly. Then she excused herself before dessert.

The next morning I found the recital program in the trash.

She didn't crumple it. Didn't tear it up. Just folded it once and dropped it in the kitchen bin, under some paper towels so I wouldn't see it unless I was taking the bag out.

I'd spent twenty minutes of our dinner dissecting one stumble in one song, ignoring three others she'd performed beautifully. I'd taken a night that was, by any reasonable measure, a success, and I'd trained her attention — and mine — on the only part that wasn't.

The praise I'd given her right after the performance? She'd forgotten it by the time we got to the car. The question about the stumble? She'll probably remember it when she's thirty.

I study this stuff for a living. I've read every paper on negativity bias in memory encoding. I've written about it, taught it, used it as a case study in talks.

And I still did it. Because knowing the bias exists doesn't mean you stop participating in it. It just means you get to feel worse later when you notice what you've done.

Here's what the research actually shows, stripped of jargon.

When you receive feedback that contains both positive and negative content, your brain processes the negative material more slowly and more thoroughly than the positive material. It gets encoded into memory with more detail. It's recalled more accurately after a delay. And — this is the part that matters most — it exerts a larger effect on your overall self-assessment than an equivalent amount of positive feedback pushes your self-assessment in the other direction.

An employee who hears ten compliments and one criticism in a performance review doesn't walk away feeling ten-elevenths good about themselves. They walk away thinking about the criticism. It recalibrates their entire sense of how they're doing in a way that the ten compliments don't recalibrate it back.

This isn't a feelings thing. It's a weighting thing.

Your brain assigns the negative comment more importance than its share of the total feedback would justify, not because you're being irrational, but because the negativity bias is doing what it evolved to do: prioritizing information about threats over information about things going fine.

A tiger in the bush is more important to notice than ten bushes with no tiger. The fact that most bushes are safe doesn't make the one dangerous bush less dangerous. The asymmetry makes sense in the wild.

The problem is that we've imported that same asymmetry into a conference room where your manager is trying to tell you about your career, and now a single two-sentence critique about a missed deadline is outweighing six months of steady, competent work in your own private accounting of whether you're good at your job.

Sarah — let's call her Sarah, because this version of the story is specific enough that it deserves a name even if the person is a composite — had worked in marketing for a mid-size software company for three years when she sat down for her annual review.

She was good at her job. Not extraordinary, not flailing. Good. The kind of reliable, second-in-command marketer who makes campaigns actually happen while the higher-ups do strategy.

Her manager came prepared. Page and a half of notes. Eleven bullet points under "What went well." One bullet under "Where we can improve."

The eleven bullets were specific and generous: a demand-gen campaign that beat its lead target by 18 percent. A messy client relationship she'd stabilized after the previous account lead quit with no notice. Two junior colleagues she'd mentored through their first campaigns. A process improvement she'd proposed — something to do with how the team reconciled spend data across platforms — that saved maybe four to six hours of manual work every week.

The one criticism: she'd missed a product launch deadline by three weeks because she'd underestimated how long a vendor would take to turn around creative assets.

Her manager spent maybe two minutes on the missed deadline out of a thirty-minute conversation. The rest was praise, context, forward-looking planning.

Sarah left the meeting able to recite the missed-deadline sentence word for word.

She couldn't, that same evening, recall more than vague shapes of the eleven positive bullets. Something about a campaign doing well. Something about mentoring. The process improvement she'd forgotten entirely until her manager mentioned it.

Over the next month, when she thought about her performance at all, she thought about the deadline. It became the organizing fact of her year. The thing that mattered. The thing she'd screwed up.

Not because her manager delivered it badly. Not because Sarah was oversensitive. But because her brain had encoded the missed deadline with ten times the depth and weight it had used for anything positive, and there's no amount of good delivery that corrects for a distortion happening entirely on the receiving end, after the words have already been heard.

You might be thinking: isn't this fixable with better communication? Clearer framing, more careful word choice, sandwiching criticism between two pieces of praise the way every management book since 1987 has recommended?

Sort of. But not really.

The problem isn't that managers are bad at delivering feedback. Some are, obviously. But even managers who are very good at it — who frame criticism constructively, who balance positive and negative content carefully, who make sure to end on an optimistic note — still run into the same problem: the recipient's brain weights the negative material more heavily than the positive material, regardless of how it's packaged.

You can soften the criticism. You can bury it in qualifiers. You can deliver it as gently as possible.

But soften it too much and the employee can't act on it. They walk out of the meeting knowing something's wrong, unable to name what, unable to fix it. Maximum emotional impact, zero practical use.

Or you can deliver the criticism more bluntly, reasoning that only a forceful statement will cut through the fog of everything positive you've already said.

But deliver it too bluntly and it detonates out of proportion to the actual performance gap. The employee spends the next three months obsessing over one comment that should've been a minor course correction, not a referendum on their competence.

Both instincts are reasonable. Both are trying to solve a real problem. And both interact with the recipient's negativity bias in ways that make the underlying distortion worse instead of better.

Kim Scott eventually figured out that the problem with her Google training program wasn't the structure of the feedback. It was the setting. A scheduled performance review, in a closed room, with your manager, creates a context where your brain is already primed to find threat. The structure itself — the thing meant to make feedback fair and consistent — is the thing that activates the bias at full strength.

A casual comment over lunch can be dismissed. A line in a formal document with your name on it, delivered by the person who controls your raise, does not get dismissed. Not because the content is more accurate, but because the setting signals importance in a way that recruits every ounce of the negativity bias's attention.

Here's what this costs in the real world, not in a lab.

Start with the person receiving the feedback — Sarah, your colleague, you. You walk out of a review with one negative comment ringing louder than ten positive ones. Over the next few weeks, that comment doesn't fade. It sharpens. You replay it. You wonder if it means more than your manager said. You start second-guessing decisions you would've made confidently last month.

If the criticism was about something visible — how you run meetings, how you communicate updates — you start overcompensating. You turn a minor note about being more concise into a policy of saying as little as possible in standups, which makes you look disengaged, which creates a new problem that wasn't there before.

Or you do the opposite: you retreat. You stop volunteering for visible projects because visible projects are where you might screw up again, and screwing up again might confirm that the one piece of criticism was actually the truth about you, and the ten pieces of praise were just your manager being nice.

Either way, the performance gap the review was meant to close doesn't close. It widens. Not because the feedback was wrong, but because the weight you assigned to it was five times heavier than anything your manager intended, and now you're solving for a problem much bigger than the one that actually exists.

Multiply that across a team of eight people, each walking out of their own review with their own distorted weighting, and you get a team that's quietly less willing to take risks, less willing to surface problems early, more likely to play it safe in ways that feel like professionalism but are actually just risk aversion born from the fear of generating another negative comment that will outweigh everything else for the next six months.

Now multiply it across an organization of two hundred people, and you get entire departments where the formal feedback system — the thing meant to help people grow — has quietly become the thing people learn to avoid, work around, or ignore, because the cost of engaging with it honestly is higher than the benefit of getting useful information about how to improve.

The manager's side isn't simpler.

You know, if you've managed anyone for more than a year, that your negative comments land harder than you intend. You've watched it happen. You've said something you thought was minor and watched the person across the table deflate like you'd just fired them.

So you learn to soften. You hedge. You bury the actual criticism so deep in qualifiers and positive framing that by the time you get to the point, the point is almost unintelligible.

"Overall I think you're doing really well, and I know this project had a lot of moving parts, and the vendor situation was tricky, but just for future planning it might be worth thinking about building in a little more buffer when we're working with external timelines."

The employee hears "you screwed up the timeline," because that's the only part of the sentence their brain is scanning for. But they can't figure out what they're supposed to do differently next time, because the actual feedback — build in more buffer — got so buried in softening that it stopped being actionable.

Or you go the other direction. You know softened feedback gets ignored, so you deliver it more forcefully. You say the thing plainly. You don't hedge.

And it lands like a grenade.

The employee spends the next month acting like they're on probation, when all you meant was "next time add two weeks to the vendor estimate."

Both strategies are rational responses to a real problem. Neither solves it. Because the problem isn't on your end of the conversation. It's on the receiving end, in how the brain encodes negative information with more weight and more permanence than positive information, and no amount of careful delivery fully compensates for that.

Some managers stop giving critical feedback altogether. Not because they don't care, but because watching it detonate out of proportion every time is exhausting, and eventually it's easier to just write "meets expectations" on everyone's review and save the real conversations for the people who are about to get fired, where the stakes are high enough that the discomfort is worth it.

Which means the employees who are doing fine — who could be doing better with one or two small course corrections — never get the feedback they need, because their manager has learned through experience that delivering it carefully still causes more damage than the benefit is worth.

You end up with a system where feedback only flows at the extremes. Glowing praise for the top performers. Serious warnings for the people on their way out. And a vast middle where nobody says anything honest, because honesty has been weaponized by a bias nobody meant to activate but everyone's participating in anyway.

Let's talk about the written record, because it makes everything worse in a way that's worth separating out.

Verbal feedback at least allows real-time correction. Your manager says something, you wince, they see the wince and immediately walk it back or add context. "I don't mean it's a big deal, I just mean let's keep an eye on it." The feedback lands closer to what was intended because there's a loop.

Written feedback has no loop.

Your manager writes the review, sends it, and you read it alone. The one critical sentence sits on the page with exactly the same visual weight as the ten positive sentences around it. You can't see your manager's face to gauge how serious they are. You can't ask a clarifying question and get an immediate answer. You can only read it, and reread it, and reread it again at two in the morning when you wake up thinking about it.

And here's the perverse part: most managers, aware that written feedback can land harder than intended, try to minimize negative points by making them brief.

One sentence. Terse. Get in and out.

The theory is that brevity signals proportion. A short sentence is a small problem. A long paragraph is a big problem.

In practice, brevity signals the opposite. A negative point compressed into one terse sentence, surrounded by longer, more elaborated positive points, doesn't read as minor. It reads as so serious the manager didn't want to elaborate. The kind of thing you say quickly because it's uncomfortable to say at all.

Sarah's manager wrote two sentences about the missed deadline. Probably because he didn't want to dwell on it. Probably because he thought two sentences, surrounded by eleven detailed positive bullets, would communicate that the deadline was a small thing in the context of a strong year.

Sarah read those two sentences as the most important part of the review. Not because she misunderstood them, but because their brevity made them feel weighty in a way the longer, more generous bullets didn't. Like a doctor saying "we need to talk" and then pausing.

The pause is worse than the words.

Let's make this concrete with something you've probably seen: the 360-degree review.

The theory behind 360s is sound. Instead of one manager's perspective — which might be skewed by their own biases, blind spots, or the fact that they only see a slice of your work — you get feedback from peers, direct reports, maybe a cross-functional collaborator or two. Average across enough perspectives and you should get something closer to the truth than any single rater could give you.

In practice, the negativity bias reasserts itself at the aggregate level in a way the averaging doesn't catch.

Let's say you get feedback from eight people. Seven of them give you strong ratings and specific, positive written comments. One — maybe a peer you had a tense exchange with during a project, or a direct report going through a rough time of their own — gives you a notably low score and writes a critical comment.

The numeric average of the eight scores will be strong, correctly reflecting that seven out of eight people were satisfied.

But you, reading the full report, don't experience it as a numeric average.

You fixate on the one low score. You read the critical comment three times. You start mentally reconstructing the interaction that must've caused it, wondering what you did wrong, planning how to repair it.

The seven strong scores? Background noise. "Most people said I'm doing fine." No detail, no weight.

The one negative score becomes the organizing fact of the review, the thing you think about when you think about how you're doing, the thing you bring up six months later when someone asks how your last review went.

One out of eight. Twelve percent of the data. Eighty percent of the emotional and cognitive weight.

This isn't because you're bad at math. It's because the negativity bias doesn't do averages. It does threat detection. And one person saying you screwed something up is a threat in a way that seven people saying you're doing fine is not a reassurance of equivalent magnitude.

Organizations that run 360s well build a countermeasure directly into the delivery process. Before handing you the raw data, a facilitator or manager frames the aggregate result: "Seven of eight raters gave you strong marks. One person's experience was different, and it's worth understanding why, but that one score doesn't erase the other seven."

It's not a complicated intervention. It's just naming the pattern before your brain has a chance to do its own weighting.

But most organizations don't do this. They hand you a spreadsheet with eight rows of scores and let you find the low one yourself.

Which you will. Immediately. Before you've read a single positive comment.

The distortion runs the other direction too.

Managers forming an overall assessment of an employee across a full year are subject to the same bias. Not just in what they choose to write down, but in what they remember as they're deciding what to write.

A year is a long time. Dozens of projects, hundreds of small interactions, a few big wins, a few mistakes. When your manager sits down in November to write your review for the year that started in January, they're not working from a comprehensive record of everything you did. They're working from memory. And memory is not a neutral recording device.

What your manager will remember most vividly: the negative incidents. The missed deadline. The tense meeting. The client complaint. The project that went sideways.

Not because they're keeping score unfairly. But because negative events generate more vivid, more detailed, more durable memories than positive events do. A missed deadline is surprising. It generates a story: what went wrong, why, what we had to do to fix it. It gets encoded with all the detail that surprise and narrative provide.

Ordinary competence doesn't generate stories. You hit your deadlines, you run your meetings, you do the work. It's smooth. Unremarkable. Forgettable.

By the time your manager sits down to write, the available material in memory is already skewed toward the negative. The year you actually had — let's say eleven months of steady, solid work and one memorable screw-up — has been compressed in their recall into something closer to "a pretty good year with that one problem."

The rating that results might be fair on average. But it's built from distorted materials. And if you happened to have one memorable negative incident in a year of otherwise fine work, while your colleague had zero memorable incidents in a year of equally fine work, you'll get a lower rating than they do — not because you performed worse, but because you generated a vivid memory in your manager's head and your colleague didn't.

The gap isn't measuring performance. It's measuring memorability. And memorability is biased.

Some companies try to fix this with contemporaneous documentation. Instead of reconstructing the year from memory, managers are asked to log incidents as they happen — both positive and negative — so that the written record at review time reflects the actual distribution of events rather than the distribution of what survived in memory.

It helps. A manager working from a log of forty incidents, thirty-six positive and four negative, has a harder time writing a review dominated by the four negative ones than a manager working purely from recall, where the four negative incidents are the only ones that made it into long-term memory with any detail intact.

But it doesn't solve the weighting problem. Even with a balanced log, the manager — and the employee — will still assign more importance to the four negative incidents than their four-out-of-forty share would justify.

The bias operates after the evidence is in, in how we weight it. Better evidence helps. It doesn't fix the scale.

Here's the cost you don't see until it's already happened: people leave.

Not the bottom performers. Not the people getting bad reviews. The people getting fine reviews. Good reviews, even. People who are, by any honest accounting, doing well.

They leave because they never felt like their work was valued. Because the only feedback they remember is critical. Because they spent two years in a job where they heard ten compliments for every one criticism, and all they can recall when someone asks them how it went is the criticism.

I've sat in exit interviews where an employee tells me they didn't feel appreciated, and I've pulled up their performance review history and shown them: strong ratings, specific praise, detailed examples of work that went well. "You got a rating of exceeds expectations two years running."

And they look at the document like they're seeing it for the first time.

Because they are, in a sense. The first time they saw it, their brain skimmed past the praise and sank its teeth into the one developmental note their manager included because you're supposed to include something developmental. That note is what they remember. That note is what they told themselves the review was about. The rest vanished.

You lose good people this way. Not because you failed to appreciate them, but because appreciation doesn't encode into memory with the same strength that criticism does, and over time the gap between what you said and what they remember becomes wide enough that they stop believing they're valued.

Which means you're now recruiting and training a replacement for someone who was doing fine, and the problem that caused them to leave — the asymmetry in how feedback gets weighted — will reassert itself with the next person unless you've built a deliberate countermeasure into how feedback gets delivered and reinforced.

Most organizations don't. They treat departures like this as mysterious one-offs. "I thought they were happy." They were happy. They just don't remember being happy, because happiness doesn't engrave itself into memory the way one uncomfortable conversation does.

So what do we do?

Not "how do we eliminate the negativity bias." We don't. It's not a bug in the system. It's the system. Your brain is working as designed when it prioritizes negative information over positive information. The asymmetry kept your ancestors alive.

The question is how we compensate for it in a setting where the asymmetry produces costs rather than benefits.

First: if you manage people, say the positive stuff more often and with more specificity than feels natural.

Not because people need constant validation. Because positive feedback vanishes from memory faster than negative feedback does, which means you need more of it just to reach parity in what actually gets retained.

One compliment does not balance one criticism in the recipient's memory, even if it balances it on your spreadsheet. You need something closer to five positive comments to offset the weight of one negative comment in how the employee experiences the overall feedback.

That feels like overkill when you're delivering it. It will feel like you're praising people for brushing their teeth.

Do it anyway.

The ratio that feels balanced to you as a manager produces an experience of constant criticism for the person receiving it, because their brain is weighting your one critical comment five times heavier than you intended.

If you want the employee to walk away with an accurate sense that they're doing well with one thing to work on, you need to give them five specific pieces of positive feedback for every one piece of critical feedback. Not because the math says so, but because their memory does.

Second: deliver positive feedback immediately, and critical feedback after a delay.

Negative feedback is going to stick whether you deliver it today or next week. It encodes deeply. It's durable. You don't need recency on your side for it to be remembered.

Positive feedback is fragile. It fades. If you wait a week to tell someone they did a great job on a presentation, the moment is gone. The work has blurred into the general sense that the project went fine. The specificity you could've anchored to — "the way you handled the VP's question about cost in slide eight was exactly right" — is no longer accessible because the presentation itself is no longer vivid in their memory.

Compliment people the day it happens. Ideally within hours.

Criticism can wait until you've had time to think about whether it's proportionate, whether it's actionable, whether the problem is recurring or one-off. The employee will remember it just as clearly a week from now. Probably more clearly, because they'll have had time to notice the pattern themselves.

Third: when you deliver a performance review that contains both positive and negative content, name the weighting problem out loud before the employee's brain has a chance to do its own math.

"I'm going to walk through eleven things that went well this year and one thing I'd like us to work on together. The one thing is real and worth talking about. It's also one thing out of twelve. I'm naming that upfront because I know how brains work — the one critical point is going to feel heavier than everything else, and I want you to know that the weight you're feeling is not the weight I'm assigning to it."

It won't eliminate the asymmetry. But it gives the employee a framework for noticing when their own brain is overweighting the negative material, which at least creates the possibility of correcting for it instead of just living inside it.

Fourth: follow up on positive feedback in writing, after the fact, even when it feels redundant.

You told someone in the hallway that they did a great job on the client presentation. Great. They've already forgotten the specifics.

Send a two-sentence email that night repeating it. "You handled the pricing question in today's call really well — the way you reframed it as a value conversation instead of a cost conversation is exactly what we need more of."

It feels unnecessary. You already said it.

But verbal feedback evaporates. Written feedback has a chance of being reread later, when the employee is spiraling over some unrelated criticism and needs a reminder that they've done things well.

You're not praising them twice for the same thing. You're giving the positive feedback a second chance to encode, because the first chance failed through no fault of yours or theirs.

Fifth: if you're on the receiving end of feedback, write down the positive stuff immediately.

You will not remember it otherwise. Your brain is going to prioritize the criticism because that's what brains do. If you want any chance of retaining an accurate picture of how you're actually doing, you need an external record that doesn't rely on memory.

Keep a document. When your manager says something positive, write it down that day. Exact words if you can. If you can't, gist plus enough detail that you'll recognize it later.

Then, when you get criticism — and you will, because everyone does — you have something to weigh it against other than your brain's distorted version of events where the criticism is the only thing that happened.

Sixth: if you're running a 360 process, frame the aggregate result before you hand over the raw data.

"Eight people gave you feedback. Seven were strong. One was notably lower. Let's talk about the one, but let's not let it erase the seven."

That's it. Ten seconds. It doesn't eliminate the employee's tendency to fixate on the one negative score, but it at least creates a competing narrative that the one score is not the whole story.

Most organizations don't do this. They treat employees like rational processors of numerical data, which we are not and have never been.

You're not managing spreadsheets. You're managing human attention, and human attention is biased. Frame the data in a way that compensates for the bias, or the data will be distorted before it ever reaches a decision.

None of this is a complete solution. There is no complete solution, because the problem is not a broken system. The problem is a feature of human cognition that we've carried into a setting where it doesn't serve us.

But we can compensate. We can build feedback cultures that account for the asymmetry instead of pretending it doesn't exist. We can say the positive stuff more often, with more detail, with more immediacy, because that's what it takes for positive feedback to survive in memory at all. We can stop treating one piece of criticism as equivalent to one piece of praise and start treating it as equivalent to five pieces of praise, because that's the actual exchange rate in the recipient's brain.

And we can stop blaming people — employees for being too sensitive, managers for being bad communicators — for a distortion that's operating on both sides of the conversation whether anyone intended it or not.

The performance review didn't break because someone ran it wrong. It broke because we built a high-stakes feedback ritual inside a species whose brains assign ten times more weight to bad news than to good news, and then we acted surprised when the ritual produced distorted outcomes.

We know better now. The research is clear. The mechanisms are documented. The fix is not complicated.

The question is whether we're willing to treat feedback like the cognitively biased process it actually is, instead of the rational exchange of information we keep pretending it could be.

Your employees are not going to remember this conversation the way you delivered it. They're going to remember it the way their brain encoded it. And their brain encoded the criticism with permanent ink and the praise with a pencil.

If you want them to remember both, you're going to need a lot more pencils.

You can quote the criticism word-for-word. The praise? Somewhere in there, probably. That asymmetry isn't a bug in your wiring—it's load-bearing.

You can quote the criticism word-for-word. The praise? Somewhere in there, probably. That asymmetry isn't a bug in your wiring. It's about to explain why your news feed looks the way it does.

Chapter 3: If It Bleeds

In 2014, Katharine Viner — not yet editor-in-chief of The Guardian, but running its U.S. digital operation — tried something her readers had been begging for. Focus groups said they wanted it. Angry emails demanded it. Comment threads beneath nearly every piece of hard news erupted with some version of the same complaint: *Why don't you ever cover anything good?*

So she launched it. Not fluff. Real reporting. A journalist embedded for three months with a literacy program in Philadelphia that was genuinely closing the achievement gap.

So she launched it. Not fluff. Real reporting. A journalist embedded for three months with a literacy program in Philadelphia that was genuinely closing the achievement gap. A deep investigation of a reentry program in Atlanta cutting recidivism in half. A profile of a Johns Hopkins researcher whose decade of unglamorous lab work had just cracked open a new treatment avenue for a rare pediatric cancer. These stories were well-written, carefully sourced, fact-checked to the same standard as the investigative pieces that built the Guardian's reputation. They got prominent homepage placement every morning.

For three months.

Almost nobody read them.

I mean — *some* people read them. Enough to register in the analytics. But nothing close to the numbers a story about a convenience store robbery in a suburb nobody'd heard of could pull in fifteen minutes. The good-news piece got skimmed. The robbery story got clicked, read to the end, shared across Twitter and

Facebook, embedded in aggregation roundups at other outlets, argued about in the comments. After three months, the good-news vertical got downgraded to once a week. Then twice a month. Then folded into a general "Community" section that also ran the robbery stories, and within six months you couldn't find it on the homepage unless you scrolled past everything else first.

Viner wasn't cynical about it. She genuinely believed her readers when they said they wanted this. And her readers weren't lying — when you asked them what they wanted to see more of, they meant it. But what people say they want in a survey and what their attention actually does when good news and bad news sit side by side on a screen are two completely different things.

The negativity bias doesn't consult stated preferences. It doesn't care what you wish you cared about. It operates in the same automatic, fast-twitch attention machinery this book opened with — the same system that made you reread the single critical comment on your presentation while skimming past ten compliments. A news homepage is maybe the most efficient testing environment ever designed for putting that machinery under load and measuring exactly what it does.

Here's what we don't talk about enough when we talk about media bias.

It's not a conspiracy. It's not, most of the time, even a conscious choice.

It's a feedback loop. And it runs at a scale, with enough real-time instrumentation, that it compounds faster than any single person inside the loop can fully see from where they're standing.

Picture a Tuesday morning budget meeting in any mid-sized newsroom — I've watched versions of this exact scene in Portland, Atlanta, Chicago, and the details barely shift. An editor sits with two story options for Wednesday's homepage. One: a local infrastructure project that came in on time and under budget. Competent work. Genuinely useful to readers who care how their tax dollars get spent. Solid reporting, no errors, cleanly written. Also, on the page, a little flat.

The other option: a permitting dispute that delayed a smaller project across town. Not a scandal. Not even especially important in the long run. But there's conflict — a contractor blaming a city official, the city official blaming the contractor back, someone clearly at fault even if the stakes are low.

She's run both kinds of stories before. She's looked at the analytics afterward. She knows, without opening a dashboard, which one will hold readers past paragraph three.

This choice doesn't require cynicism. It doesn't require malice, or a secret agenda to make the world look worse than it is. It requires only an editor doing her job — trying to get the story read — informed by an honest track record of what readers actually do instead of what they say they want.

When that choice gets repeated across thousands of editors making thousands of similar calls every single day, the accumulated result is a news environment that skews measurably, systematically negative relative to the actual distribution of events it's covering. Not because anyone set out to make it that way. Because every single reasonable individual decision, made inside a system that rewards one kind of attention over another, pushed in the same direction.

And before someone says this is a digital-era problem — a consequence of clickthrough metrics and A/B testing and the speed of the internet — let me stop you.

Newspaper competition in the 1890s produced front pages that leaned hard into crime, scandal, disaster, threat. Joseph Pulitzer and William Randolph Hearst didn't have clickthrough data. They had only the blunt instrument of daily circulation numbers, updated once a day instead of once a second. Even that coarse a signal was enough to push coverage in the exact same direction it's been pushed ever since.

The technology changed. The selection pressure didn't.

Because the selection pressure was never about the technology. It was about the audience's attention, running on the same negativity-biased machinery in an 1895 newsstand line as in a 2026 doomscroll.

I want to be careful here.

The easy version of this argument — the one you hear at dinner parties from people who've just discovered media criticism — is that journalists cynically manufacture bad news because it sells. That's not what I'm saying.

Most of the journalists I know (and I know a fair number; I spent three years covering municipal budget hearings and zoning disputes before figuring out I was better suited to writing books than filing daily) got into this work because they care about accuracy, accountability, serving the public good. Most editors I've talked to about this genuinely struggle with the gap between what they want to cover and what their metrics tell them people will actually read.

They're not villains. They're people trying to keep a newsroom funded in an environment where every story's performance gets measured in real time, and the ones that don't perform don't get repeated.

The problem isn't individual bad actors.

The problem is a system where every individual good-faith actor, responding to real feedback about what's working, ends up compounding a bias none of them would endorse if you described it to them in the aggregate.

Researchers have tested this directly. They've shown people matched pairs of headlines — same underlying event, one framed positively, one framed negatively — and measured which one gets clicked. Negative framing wins. Consistently. Even when the actual newsworthiness of the story is identical.

They've run studies where they ask people beforehand which kind of headline they expect to prefer — and people predict, sincerely, that they'll choose the positive one. Then the researchers actually show them the headlines under normal reading conditions (not in a survey where you're consciously thinking about your answer), and the same people click the negative headline at rates well above what they predicted.

The mismatch isn't a fluke. It shows up across formats, across countries, across the whole messy transition from print to digital. It replicates in every well-designed study I've seen. Which suggests the underlying mechanism isn't about a particular platform or a particular culture or a particular era's editors making worse choices than they used to.

It's about general-purpose human attention machinery, now expressed through news consumption instead of product reviews or workplace feedback.

The bias doesn't change. Only the domain changes.

Let me tell you what this looks like when it runs long enough to compound.

Violent crime in the United States peaked in 1991. From that peak, it fell — not a little, but dramatically. More than half over the next two decades. The murder rate dropped by close to fifty percent between 1991 and 2014, depending on which dataset you use. Other rich countries saw similar drops over similar timeframes. This wasn't a blip. It was a generation-long trend, sustained across multiple economic cycles, multiple presidential administrations, measurable in every serious dataset criminologists track.

During that same period, if you polled Americans about whether crime was rising or falling in their own neighborhood, most said falling. They could see it. They felt safer walking to the corner store after dark, letting their kids play outside unsupervised, the everyday texture of life in a place that had gotten measurably less violent.

But if you asked those same people whether crime *nationally* was going up or down, most said up.

Consistently.

Year after year.

Even as the national rate kept falling.

This is the signature of the compounding loop this chapter is about. It's not that people are stupid, or uninformed, or watching the wrong cable news channel. It's that the information environment they're drawing from — across channels, across outlets, even across the supposedly "good" sources that care about accuracy — is systematically overrepresenting violent crime relative to its actual frequency. Because violent crime is vivid, dramatic, emotionally chargeable in exactly the way the negativity bias is tuned to prioritize.

Coverage volume for violent crime tracks how alarming and mentally available the category is, not how often it actually happens.

And when that disparity runs for long enough, it trains public perception more forcefully than the underlying statistics can update it.

Here's what I mean. A person doing everything right by the usual standards — reading widely, checking multiple sources, avoiding the obvious partisan rags, maybe even looking at the actual FBI crime reports once or twice a year — can still come away with a distorted sense of the trendline. Not because any individual source lied to them. Because the distortion isn't a property of any one source's dishonesty.

It's a property of which stories, among the accurate ones available, get selected and amplified by a system responding to the same attention asymmetry in every individual case.

Think about what that means for a second. You can be well-informed — genuinely, honestly well-informed by conventional standards — and still carry around a mental model of the world that's systematically skewed in one direction. Because "well-informed" usually means you've read a lot of news, and if the news you're reading is itself selected from a skewed sample, reading more of it just compounds the skew.

It's like trying to fix a crooked picture by stepping farther back. You see more of the wall, but the picture's still crooked.

Here's the part that costs us. The part I don't think we've fully reckoned with yet.

When your perception of the world runs systematically ahead of the actual danger in it, you don't just feel worse.

You make different choices. Worse choices, in a lot of cases, because you're solving for a threat level that isn't real.

I know parents — good parents, thoughtful people — who remember playing outside unsupervised as kids in the 1980s and early '90s. Riding bikes to friends' houses three miles away. Walking to school alone in second grade. Spending whole summer afternoons at the park with nothing but a quarter for the pay phone in case of emergency. They remember this fondly. Many of them credit that freedom with teaching them independence, resilience, how to navigate conflict without an adult stepping in to mediate every dispute.

And now those same parents won't let their own kids do any of it.

Not because their neighborhood got more dangerous. It got *safer*, measurably safer, by every metric that matters. But the perceived danger — fed by two decades of cable news and Amber Alerts and viral crime stories shared across Facebook — looms larger in their minds than the actual risk looms in reality.

The statistics say stranger abduction (the scenario most parents fear when they think about their kid walking to school alone) is vanishingly rare, lower now than it was in 1980. But the coverage volume for the cases that do happen has gone up, because each case now gets national attention instead of local, and because the format of modern news — 24-hour cable, social media, push notifications — ensures that a single abduction story can be re-reported, re-shared, re-traumatized across multiple news cycles until it feels like an epidemic even when it's an isolated tragedy.

So we get a generation of kids who are statistically safer than their parents were, but practically more constrained. Driven to school instead of walking. Supervised at the park instead of left to figure out the slide hierarchy on their own. Raised in a world that *feels* more dangerous than the world their parents navigated at the same age, even though the numbers say the opposite.

And the kids notice. They internalize it.

I've watched this happen. A friend's daughter, nine years old, smart kid, asks why she's not allowed to walk the four blocks to her friend's house when her mom used to walk twice that distance at the same age. The mom explains — carefully, because she's trying to be honest without scaring her kid — that the world's different now. More dangerous. You have to be careful.

Except it's not more dangerous. It's *less* dangerous. The mom believes what she's saying, but what she believes is a distortion produced by the same attention machinery that's been compounding in her news feed for twenty years. And now she's passing that distortion to her daughter, who's learning that the world outside the car, outside the supervised playdate, outside the adult-mediated zone, is too dangerous to be trusted.

Which means the daughter doesn't get the same chances her mother got to practice independence in low-stakes environments where the cost of a mistake is a scraped knee instead of (I don't know) a failed first semester of college because you never learned how to manage your own time.

I'm not saying we should be careless. I'm not saying stranger danger is a myth or that all parental caution is overblown.

I'm saying the gap between perception and reality has a cost. And the cost isn't borne equally by the people whose attention created the gap in the first place.

The nine-year-old doesn't get a vote on whether the threat model her parents are operating from is accurate. She just inherits the constraints it produces. And learns, in the process, that the world is scarier than it actually is — not because anyone lied to her, but because the information environment her parents trusted was itself running on a selection bias none of them could see from the inside.

Here's another cost, bigger and harder to measure but visible if you squint at the right datasets.

Voters demand tougher sentencing, harsher enforcement, less investment in rehabilitation, because they're operating from a mental model where crime is spiking and the system is failing. Even when the system, by most measurable outcomes, has been working better than it has in half a century.

Three-strikes laws passed in the mid-1990s, right around the peak of the crime wave, made sense to an electorate that believed the threat was accelerating. But those same laws stayed on the books — and in many states, got harsher — well into the 2000s and 2010s, even as the crime rate that justified them kept falling.

Because the perceived threat, the one reflected in news coverage and voter surveys and campaign ads, didn't fall at anything like the same rate the actual crime rate did.

Think about what that means in practice. A person convicted of a third nonviolent offense in 1997, when the murder rate was still relatively high and public fear was running hot, might get a sentence that makes sense given the context. The same person convicted of the same three offenses in 2012, when the murder rate had dropped by nearly half, gets the same sentence — or longer, because some states ratcheted the penalties up in the intervening years — even though the underlying risk to public safety has changed dramatically.

The law didn't update to reflect the new reality because the public's perception of the reality didn't update. And the public's perception didn't update because the information environment they were drawing from kept serving them the same mental model, compounded by fifteen more years of selection bias favoring the stories that made crime feel urgent and present and escalating.

We've professionalized fault-finding to the point where an entire generation has learned to weigh bad news at ten times its actual mass.

And the cost isn't just pessimism.

It's paralysis. It's polarization — because if you genuinely believe the world is falling apart, compromise starts to look like surrender, and the people on the other side of the compromise start to look like threats rather than fellow citizens with different priors. It's a society that can't hear good news even when it's screaming, because the good news has to fight through an information environment engineered (inadvertently, but inexorably) to bury it.

I'm not saying the world is fine. It's not. There are real problems, real threats, real injustices that deserve urgent attention and resources and the kind of sustained investigative journalism that holds power to account when it would rather not be held. I don't want a media that stops covering those things.

I want a media that covers them in proportion to their actual frequency and severity instead of in proportion to how much they activate our threat-detection machinery.

But when the same negativity bias that helps us spot real problems also makes us overweight them, overestimate their frequency, and underestimate the progress we've actually made on the ones we've been working on for decades, we end up with a public that's exhausted, cynical, and increasingly unable to distinguish between a real crisis and the fiftieth overheated headline about a modest setback.

The newsrooms that have tried to correct for this — honestly, deliberately, with real resources behind the effort — have learned something useful, even if the overall lesson is humbling.

Pure good-news coverage, the kind disconnected from any specific problem it's addressing, performs poorly. Readers don't come back to it. It doesn't hold attention. It doesn't get shared.

This is what Katharine Viner learned at the Guardian. It's what NPR learned when it tried a similar experiment in 2016. It's what the Solutions Journalism Network — a nonprofit founded specifically to study and promote better models for covering what works, not just what fails — has confirmed across dozens of partner outlets over the last decade.

If you're fighting the negativity bias head-on, on the terms of "good news versus bad news," you lose. Every time.

But.

There's a second finding. Quieter, more durable, visible in the data from the outlets that stuck with it long enough to iterate instead of giving up after the first three months.

Coverage that pairs a specific, real problem with a documented, credible response to that problem — not manufactured uplift, but an honest account of what actually worked, reported with the same rigor you'd bring to a disaster story — performs considerably better than context-free positivity. Not as well as a straight negative story, usually. But well enough to justify the resources. And well enough, over time, to start shifting the overall mix.

Let me give you an example.

In 2018, Jennifer Sullivan, a reporter at the Seattle Times, wrote a piece about homelessness. But instead of the usual angle — encampment sweep, public health crisis, neighborhood complaints — she focused on a specific pilot program placing chronically homeless people directly into permanent housing without requiring them to get sober or employed first. The model's called Housing First, and it had been tested in other cities with mixed but generally promising results.

Sullivan's piece didn't ignore the costs or the controversy. She interviewed people who thought the program was a waste of taxpayer money. She reported on the logistics, the budget, the failure rate for people who couldn't sustain the housing even with support. She didn't pretend it was a magic solution.

But the core of the story was about what actually worked. Which parts of the program were producing measurable reductions in emergency room visits, police calls, shelter stays. Which practices the pilot-city data suggested were worth scaling. What the people running the program had learned from the cases that didn't work.

The story performed well. Not viral, but well above the newsroom's average for time-on-page and shares.

More importantly, it performed well enough that Sullivan's editor greenlit a follow-up six months later, tracking the same program's expansion and documenting what happened when the model hit a larger population. And that follow-up also performed well. Which led to a third piece. And by the time Sullivan had written five or six stories in this vein, all focused on the same problem but different facets of the response to it, the data was showing something her editor hadn't expected.

Readers were coming back. Not in huge numbers, but reliably. They wanted to know what happened next.

That's the thing about solutions journalism when it's done right. It's not feel-good puffery. It's a story structure that engages the same threat-detection machinery that makes disaster stories compelling (because it establishes the stakes of the problem first) but then gives you a resolution that's grounded in evidence instead of speculation or despair.

The negativity bias doesn't disappear just because you're writing about a solution. But you're working with it instead of pretending it doesn't exist.

Here's the catch, though. And it's a big one.

Solutions journalism requires twice the reporting. You have to document the problem rigorously enough to establish credibility, and you have to document the response with the same rigor so it doesn't read like PR. That's more time, more sources, more fact-checking, more editor oversight. For a story that — even in the best-case scenario — still won't perform as well as a simpler, cheaper disaster story would.

Which means it requires editors to hold space for a kind of story their metrics are always going to undervalue relative to the alternative.

And it requires readers to notice when an outlet is actually doing this work, and to reward it with attention, subscriptions, the kind of sustained engagement that tells an editor this is worth the investment.

Most readers don't do that. Not because they're lazy or indifferent, but because the same attention machinery that makes disaster stories so compelling also makes it hard to notice when an outlet is trying to correct for the bias. The disaster story still *feels* more urgent. Still pulls harder. Still gets the click.

So the correction has to fight uphill against the same force it's trying to correct for. Which is why most attempts at solutions journalism either fade after a few months (like the Guardian's good-news vertical) or get relegated to a niche section that doesn't affect the overall mix of what shows up on the homepage.

But here's what I think we're missing when we treat this as purely a media problem.

The feedback loop that produces a negatively skewed news environment isn't just about what journalists choose to cover. It's about what we choose to read. What we click. What we share. What we talk about at dinner. What we remember a week later when someone asks if we saw anything interesting in the news.

Every one of those choices feeds back into the system that decides what gets covered next. And if we keep clicking the disaster story while scrolling past the infrastructure-project-that-came-in-under-budget story, we're training the algorithm (and the editor watching the algorithm) to give us more disasters.

Not because the editor wants to make us miserable. Because the editor's job is to give us what we demonstrably pay attention to, and we demonstrably pay more attention to bad news than good.

Which means the correction — if there's going to be one — can't come only from the supply side.

It has to come from the demand side too.

So here's what that looks like in practice.

Next time you're scrolling a news site or your social feed, notice which headlines pull you in. Notice whether the ones you click are systematically skewed toward threat, conflict, failure, disaster. Notice whether you're reading the negative stories all the way through while skimming the positive ones.

You don't have to stop reading the negative stories. Some of them are important. Some of them deserve your full attention and whatever action follows from being informed.

But if you notice the skew — if you catch yourself reflexively clicking the story about what went wrong while ignoring the story about what went right — you can make a different choice. You can deliberately click the positive story. Read it all the way through. Share it if it's worth sharing. Leave a comment. Do the small, low-cost things that signal to the system: *This is worth covering. I want more of this.*

It sounds small. It is small. One person's clicks aren't going to reshape the entire information environment.

But the information environment isn't shaped by one person. It's shaped by millions of people making the same small choice, compounded over time, in the same direction.

Right now, those choices are compounding in favor of negativity. Not because we're bad people, but because we're running on machinery that was shaped in an environment where threats were more urgent than opportunities, and we haven't yet figured out how to recalibrate for an environment where the threat level and the information volume are wildly out of proportion.

The recalibration doesn't happen automatically. It doesn't happen just because we wish it would, or because we tell a pollster we want more good news.

It happens when we notice the machinery doing what it does, and we deliberately choose to do something different.

That's not the whole solution. Not even close. The structural problems with how news gets funded and produced and distributed are real, and they're not going to be fixed by individual readers making slightly different clicking choices.

But it's a start. And it's the part we actually control.

The negativity bias is general-purpose. It runs whether we're reading news or performance reviews or online product ratings. But the *expression* of that bias — how much it skews our perception, how much it costs us in missed opportunities and distorted threat models and nine-year-olds who don't get to walk to school — depends on how we respond to it once we notice it's there.

We can keep letting it run unchecked, clicking every disaster story and skimming every success story, and watch the gap between perception and reality keep widening.

Or we can start treating our attention like the signal it is. Deliberately. Consistently. In full knowledge that the machinery pulling us toward bad news is never going to stop pulling, but that we don't have to follow every pull just because we feel it.

The machinery doesn't get a vote on what we do next.

We do.

The Guardian's Good News Project failed because 'if it bleeds, it leads' isn't a newsroom slogan—it's a user behavior pattern, a measured fact about what we say we want versus what we actually click.

The Good News Project proved readers don't actually want what they say they want—or can't choose it even when they do. That's individuals clicking one headline at a time. But the asymmetry doesn't stop at personal preference. It shapes the systems we build to measure what matters.

Chapter 4: The Gottman Ratio

It takes five good interactions to outweigh one bad one. Not four. Not ‘more good than bad.’ Five to one. That’s the ratio John Gottman found after watching hundreds of couples in what he called the Love Lab, and it’s the measured price of staying married when you’re human. The couples whose marriages lasted didn’t fight less or avoid conflict. They just made five deposits for every withdrawal, every single time, or the account went negative and stayed there.

The pattern that emerged wasn’t what most people expect.

The couples whose marriages lasted didn’t fight less. They didn’t avoid conflict. What separated them from the couples heading toward divorce was a ratio—a lopsided, almost absurd ratio of positive interactions to negative ones. Not one-to-one. Not even two-to-one. The stable couples were running at something closer to five positive interactions for every negative one just to hold steady.

Think about that. Five to one. Not to thrive. Just to not deteriorate.

If you’re reading that number and it sounds high, you’re responding the way most people do when they first encounter Gottman’s research. It feels like overkill. If negative and positive interactions carried equal weight, a relationship running even slightly positive—say, three good exchanges for every bad one—should feel comfortably ahead. It doesn’t work that way. And the reason it doesn’t work that way is exactly what the previous chapters have been building toward: negative interactions are not processed, remembered, or felt with anything close to the same weight as positive ones. A single sharp criticism during an argument doesn’t just sit in memory alongside the compliment from that morning, equally weighted, waiting to be canceled out. It gets more attention when it happens.

More rehearsal afterward as your mind keeps returning to it. A sharper, more durable place in memory once it's fully encoded. The negative interaction is doing more work per instance than the positive one ever could.

I've watched this play out in my own life more times than I'd like to admit. A day that objectively contained ten pleasant exchanges and one tense one doesn't feel like a 10-to-1 day when I'm lying in bed that night replaying it. It feels like the day that tense exchange happened, with the pleasant stuff blurred into background. My wife and I can spend a whole weekend together—laughing over breakfast, taking a long walk, cooking dinner while trading stories about our week—and if we have one fifteen-minute argument about whose turn it was to take the trash out, that fifteen minutes is what I'll remember most vividly a month later. Not because the argument was objectively more important. Because it *felt* heavier in the moment, and that subjective weight is what memory preserves.

Gottman's five-to-one ratio isn't an arbitrary cultural preference for niceness. It's closer to a compensation figure. The amount of positive material a relationship needs to generate just to offset the built-in handicap that every negative interaction already carries, regardless of how much the two people actually love each other underneath it all.

Here's what makes this even more maddening: the negative interactions that do the most damage aren't the ones most couples think they need to worry about.

Ordinary disagreement—"I wish you'd told me you were running late," "I don't think we should spend that much on a couch right now"—doesn't predict relationship failure. Couples who never disagree about anything are often *less* stable than couples who argue regularly, because suppressed conflict has its own corrosive effects that just take longer to show up. What predicts divorce, in Gottman's data, is a much smaller set of behaviors he and his team came to call the Four Horsemen: contempt, criticism (aimed at character rather than behavior), defensiveness, and stonewalling.

Contempt is the worst of the four. Not just the strongest predictor—the *single strongest* predictor Gottman's research identified. Contempt is communicating, through tone or words or just a well-timed eye roll, that you are superior to your partner. That they are beneath you. That the thing they just said or did confirms what you already suspected about their character.

I saw this once at a dinner party, and I've never forgotten it. A couple we knew—married maybe eight years at that point—were telling a story together about a trip they'd taken. The husband was doing most of the talking, getting a detail wrong about which day something happened, and his wife cut in: "No, babe, you always do this—you can't keep a timeline straight to save your life." The words alone weren't that bad. The tone was *dripping* with contempt. She wasn't correcting him. She was letting everyone at the table know she'd been dealing with his incompetence for years and had long since stopped being surprised by it.

They divorced two years later.

Contempt works on memory the same way a deeply threatening piece of news works on a newsroom: it takes up space far beyond its actual duration. A thirty-second exchange laced with contempt doesn't get stored as thirty seconds of relationship history, equally weighted against the thirty pleasant minutes that came before it. It gets stored as *evidence*—evidence of how your partner really sees you, evidence of the disrespect you're living with, evidence that gets pulled up and replayed every time you're trying to assess whether this relationship is actually working. One contemptuous moment can outweigh hours of ordinary kindness, not because the kindness doesn't matter, but because contempt is doing a different kind of work inside your memory. It's diagnostic. It tells you something you believe you need to know about who this person is when the mask slips.

Criticism aimed at character works the same way. "You're so selfish" hits harder and sticks longer than "It bothered me when you forgot to call." The first one is a claim about who your partner *is*—a stable, defining trait. The second is a claim about what they *did*—a specific, fixable behavior. Your brain treats those two claims completely differently, even when they're describing the same incident, because one feels like information about the relationship's foundation and the other feels like information about a bad Tuesday. The character-level criticism gets weighted more heavily, remembered more vividly, and integrated into your ongoing sense of whether this relationship is safe or whether you're living with someone who fundamentally doesn't respect you.

Defensiveness and stonewalling work as amplifiers. Defensiveness—meeting your partner's complaint with a counter-complaint or an excuse rather than any acknowledgment at all—turns an ordinary grievance into a fight about who's allowed to have grievances in the first place. Stonewalling—withdrawing entirely, shutting down, refusing to engage even in silence—communicates that the conversation isn't worth having, which your partner's brain tends to interpret as *you're* not worth engaging with. Both behaviors take a conflict that might have been resolvable and convert it into something that feels, to the person on the receiving end, like rejection.

The negativity bias doesn't distinguish between "my partner is having a bad day and handling this poorly" and "my partner just revealed something essential about how they see me." It just codes the whole interaction as threat-relevant and files it accordingly.

What couples—and the therapists working with them—get wrong most often is thinking that the fix is simply adding more positive interactions to the pile.

This is the same mistake the previous chapter's managers made when they tried to offset a harsh performance review by starting the next one with compliments. It doesn't work, because the negative material and the positive material aren't actually competing on the same scale inside memory. A partner who is warm, generous, and affectionate most of the time but occasionally responds to conflict with contempt is not accumulating a bank of goodwill that automatically neutralizes the contemptuous moments when the ledger gets totaled up at the end of the month. The contempt gets processed and weighted according to its own outsized rules, largely independent of how many pleasant, unremarkable days surrounded it.

I know a couple—friends of ours for years—who went through a version of this that nearly ended their marriage. The husband, by any outside measure, was a devoted partner. He cooked dinner most nights. He remembered anniversaries, planned thoughtful trips, showed up for his wife emotionally when she was going through a hard stretch at work. But about once a month, during an argument, he'd get defensive in a way that crossed a line—he'd accuse her of "always" criticizing him, bring up something she'd done wrong six months ago as a counter-move, refuse to acknowledge that her original complaint might have been legitimate. Those moments, maybe five or six per year, were reorganizing her entire felt sense of the marriage. She could *intellectually* recognize that he was a good partner most of the time. But the feeling she carried around day to day was shaped far more by those handful of defensive blow-ups than by the accumulated hundred small kindnesses in between.

When they finally went to therapy, the therapist didn't tell him to cook more dinners or plan more trips. She told him he had to stop getting defensive during conflict, full stop. Not reduce it. Not balance it out with extra niceness. *Stop doing it.* Because as long as those moments kept happening, no amount of additional positive material was going to move the ratio enough to change how the marriage actually felt from the inside.

That's the piece most people miss when they first hear about Gottman's five-to-one ratio. The ratio isn't a recipe for generating more compliments or date nights, though those things matter. It's a description of what's required to offset the damage that negative interactions *are already doing* just by existing. You can't out-compliment contempt. You have to stop being contemptuous.

Gottman's research focused on married couples, observed over years, which is where the ratio finding has been most thoroughly tested and replicated. But the mechanism isn't specific to marriage. It shows up in every relationship sustained through repeated interactions rather than a single defining event.

Friendships work the same way. A close friend cancels plans on you at the last minute—something came up, they're genuinely sorry, it wasn't malicious. You say it's fine. And maybe it is fine, intellectually. But the friendship doesn't just bounce back to where it was the day before they canceled. It feels slightly off for a while. Not broken, just... cooler. And if you pay attention to what happens next, you'll notice that the friendship doesn't return to its previous warmth until you've had several *good* interactions to counterbalance that one bad one. A long conversation where you both laughed. A favor they did for you without being asked. A moment where they showed up in a way that reminded you why you're friends in the first place.

That's the ratio operating outside of marriage. The friend who intuitively understands this will over-invest in repair after a lapse—they'll text you a few days later suggesting coffee, or send you a link to something they know you'd find funny, or just check in more often than usual for a week or two. They're not consciously calculating a five-to-one ratio. They're responding to the same felt sense you are: that one negative interaction has shifted the friendship's temperature, and it's going to take more than one positive interaction to shift it back.

The friends who *don't* understand this tend to assume that simply not repeating the offense will be sufficient. "I apologized, we're good, right?" But good-in-theory and good-in-felt-experience are not the same thing, and the negativity bias is operating on felt experience. The canceled plan is still sitting in your memory with more weight than the apology carried, and it's going to sit there until enough new positive material has accumulated to genuinely shift the balance.

Sibling relationships, parent-adult child relationships, even some work partnerships that matter enough to feel personal—they all run on versions of the same ratio. The relationships that survive occasional rough patches are the ones where both people, consciously or not, understand that repair isn't just about apology. It's about generating enough subsequent positive interactions to actually move the needle on what the relationship feels like day-to-day, because one negative interaction—especially a sharp one—isn't going to be outweighed by one positive one of equivalent size. It's going to take several.

Here's a question worth sitting with: if the ratio is real, and if it's this lopsided, why don't more relationships just collapse under the weight of accumulated negativity?

Some do, obviously. Gottman's research is full of couples who started at a healthy ratio and then slipped—sometimes slowly, sometimes suddenly—into territory where the negative interactions were happening often enough, or the positive ones rarely enough, that the ratio crossed some invisible threshold and the relationship began to feel, from the inside, like it was failing. Once that feeling takes hold, it's hard to reverse, because the negativity bias creates a feedback loop: you're now primed to notice and remember the next negative interaction even more sharply, because it's confirming what you're already starting to believe about where this is headed.

But most relationships *don't* collapse. And the reason they don't collapse is that most people, most of the time, are intuitively doing something that interrupts the negativity bias before it fully completes its work.

Gottman's team called it *repair*.

Repair, in this context, doesn't mean fixing the underlying issue that caused the conflict. It means taking a specific, deliberate action—sometimes small—during or shortly after a negative interaction to de-escalate it and re-establish connection before the interaction finishes calcifying into the kind of sharp, durable memory an unrepaired negative interaction becomes.

A well-timed joke that breaks the tension in the middle of an argument. A partner reaching across the table to touch your hand, even while you're still upset with each other. Someone saying, out loud, "Let's start this over" or "That came out harsher than I meant it" before the fight spirals further. An acknowledgment—quick, sincere, not defensive—that you just handled something poorly and you know it.

These are all forms of repair. And what makes repair so effective is that it interrupts the negativity bias's encoding process before the process fully completes. A negative interaction that gets repaired, especially if the repair happens relatively soon after the initial event, appears to get stored in memory differently than one left to sit unaddressed. Not erased—the couples in Gottman's studies who repaired well still *remembered* their conflicts. But the memory sits there with less charge. It feels more like a resolved piece of relationship history than like a live, recurring source of grievance.

Timing matters more than most people realize. A repair attempted in the middle of an escalating argument, while both people are still physiologically flooded—heart racing, adrenaline up, thinking narrowed—frequently fails to land. The same attentional machinery that makes the negative interaction so memorable in the first place also makes you less able, in that moment, to register a repair attempt as sincere rather than as a tactic to shut you up and end the conflict prematurely.

Gottman's research on physiological arousal during conflict found that couples who took a deliberate pause once either partner's heart rate crossed a certain threshold—usually somewhere around 100 beats per minute, well above normal resting rate—and then resumed the conversation only after both had calmed down enough to actually hear each other again, had far more successful repairs than couples who pushed through to what felt like resolution while still in fight-or-flight mode.

This is not intuitive. The intuitive move, when you're in the middle of a fight, is to keep going until you reach some kind of resolution, because stopping in the middle feels like avoidance or like you're letting the other person off the hook. But if you're trying to repair while you're still flooded, the repair almost never works. Your partner hears your words through the same threat-detection filter that made the original interaction feel so large, and what you meant as repair gets interpreted as defensiveness or dismissal or an attempt to win the argument rather than actually reconnect.

The couples who get good at repair learn to recognize when they've crossed that threshold—when their heart is racing, when their thinking has narrowed to the point where they're just defending their position rather than actually listening—and they *stop*. Not forever. Just long enough to let their nervous system downshift. Twenty minutes, sometimes. An hour. Long enough that when they come back to the conversation, the repair attempt can actually land the way it was intended.

One more wrinkle, and then we'll pull this toward something you can actually use.

When a conflict happens inside a relationship, one or both people will often describe it afterward to someone outside the relationship. A friend. A sibling. A parent. This is normal, healthy even—talking through a hard moment with someone who cares about you is one of the ways we process difficulty without letting it fester.

But the version that gets told inherits the same asymmetry this whole chapter has been tracing. The story your friend hears is disproportionately the sharp, memorable, negatively charged version, because that's the version sitting most vividly in your own memory when you go to tell it. You're not lying. You're not even exaggerating, necessarily. You're just recounting the version your memory preserved, which is already weighted toward the negative.

Your friend almost never hears an equally detailed account of the preceding several weeks of ordinary, affectionate cohabitation, because ordinary weeks don't generate the kind of replayable detail that makes for good storytelling or that you even *have* readily available to offer. So your friend forms an impression of your relationship that's skewed in exactly the way your own memory is skewed—toward the conflicts, the rough patches, the moments that felt threatening or hurtful enough to be worth encoding in high definition.

Over time, this creates a strange dynamic where the people who care about you most and are trying to support you through relationship difficulty are working from an incomplete, negatively weighted data set. They know about the fight you had last week. They don't know about the twenty unremarkable, perfectly fine days that came before it, because you didn't call them to report that Tuesday was pleasant.

This matters because those outside voices feed back into how you assess the relationship yourself. If everyone you trust keeps hearing your conflict stories and responding with concern—"Are you okay?" "That doesn't sound healthy"—it reinforces the interpretation your negativity-biased memory is already pushing you toward: that this relationship is in trouble, that the conflicts are the *real* story and the good days are just filler in between.

Sometimes that interpretation is correct. Sometimes the relationship *is* in trouble, and your friends are picking up on something real. But sometimes the interpretation is an artifact of the same ratio problem Gottman identified in his lab: a relationship that contains far more positive interactions than negative ones, but where the negative ones are carrying so much weight that they've reorganized everyone's sense—yours and your friends'—of what this relationship actually is.

So what do we do with this?

If you're in a relationship that matters to you—marriage, friendship, a partnership that's close enough to feel personal—here's what Gottman's research and the negativity bias framework together suggest you should actually be tracking:

First: **the ratio is real, and you can't cheat it.** A relationship running at one-to-one positive and negative interactions is not a relationship that feels balanced. It's a relationship that feels like it's losing ground, because the negative interactions are outweighing the positive ones in felt experience even when the numbers say they're even. You need a genuine, lopsided excess of positive interactions just to keep the relationship feeling stable, let alone good. If you're keeping a mental tally and thinking "we had two good days and one bad day this week, that's net positive," your tally is missing the point. The one bad day is probably outweighing the two good ones, because that's how the mechanism works.

Second: **volume is not the same as ratio.** Adding more positive interactions helps, but only if you're also addressing whatever specific negative patterns are eating up your ratio budget in the first place. If you're warm and generous most of the time but occasionally contemptuous during conflict, the fix is not more warmth—it's *stop being contemptuous.* This is harder, obviously. Changing an ingrained conflict pattern is harder than cooking an extra nice dinner or planning a surprise date. But the nice dinner isn't going to offset contempt, because contempt and niceness aren't competing on the same scale in memory. You have to actually interrupt the behavior that's creating the outsize negative weight.

Third: **repair is a skill, not an instinct, and most of us are terrible at it.** The natural response when you've just said something harsh to someone you love is to either double down and defend yourself or to withdraw into silence and wait for the whole thing to blow over. Neither of those is repair. Repair is active, immediate, and vulnerable. It's saying "I'm sorry, that was too harsh" *while the interaction is still happening*, not three days later when you've both moved on. It's reaching for your partner's hand in the middle of the argument to signal that you're still on the same team even though you're upset with each other right now. It's breaking the tension with humor, if humor is something the two of you can access in that moment, or just saying out loud "I don't want to fight about this, can we start over?"

And repair has to happen *before you've both calmed down enough that you can think clearly again.* If you're still in fight-or-flight—heart racing, thinking narrowed, words coming out sharper than you mean them—your repair attempts won't land. Take a break. Twenty minutes. An hour. Let your nervous system downshift. Then come back and try again.

Fourth: **the felt temperature of a relationship is not the same as its objective health, and the gap between those two things is where the negativity bias does its most invisible damage.** A relationship can be objectively strong—compatible values, shared life, genuine affection, all the pieces in place—and still *feel* like it's failing if the ratio has slipped far enough that the negative interactions are dominating your felt sense of what being in this relationship is like day-to-day. When that happens, the fix is not to talk yourself into seeing the relationship more positively or to remind yourself of all the good things your partner does. The fix is to *actually shift the ratio*—fewer high-charge negative interactions, more genuine positive ones, and better repair when conflicts do happen.

This is not about pretending everything is fine when it isn't. If the relationship has real, structural problems—mismatched life goals, betrayed trust, patterns that have gone on too long to repair—no amount of ratio management is going to save it, and you shouldn't try. But a lot of relationships that *feel* like they're failing are actually just running at a ratio that's slipped below what the negativity bias requires to keep the felt experience aligned with the objective reality. And those relationships can be pulled back, if both people understand what they're actually trying to fix.

Here's what I keep coming back to: the ratio isn't arbitrary. It's not a social norm or a therapeutic ideal. It's a description of what human memory actually requires, given the asymmetry already baked into how we process negative versus positive information, just to experience a relationship as stable rather than deteriorating.

Five to one sounds like overkill until you sit with what it's offsetting. One contemptuous remark, unrepaired, sitting in memory with five times the weight of a compliment. One defensive blow-up carrying more charge than a week of pleasant evenings. One friendship lapse requiring multiple subsequent good interactions before the friendship's temperature returns to where it was.

We don't get to choose whether the negativity bias operates in our relationships. It's already operating, every day, in every interaction that matters enough to be remembered. What we get to choose is whether we're going to keep pretending that one bad interaction and one good interaction cancel each other out and wondering why our relationships feel harder than the objective facts suggest they should, or whether we're going to take the ratio seriously and build relationships that actually compensate for the weight negative interactions are already guaranteed to carry.

The couples in Gottman's lab who stayed married weren't the ones who avoided conflict. They were the ones who understood, consciously or not, that every negative interaction creates a debt that has to be actively repaid—not with apologies alone, but with enough subsequent positive interactions and enough successful repair to actually move the needle on what the relationship feels like from the inside.

That's the work. Not pretending the ratio doesn't exist. Not assuming good intentions are enough to offset bad moments. Actually doing the math, and then doing the repair, and then generating enough genuine positive material to keep the ratio where it needs to be for the relationship to feel, day-to-day, like something worth protecting.

And if you're reading this and thinking "five-to-one still sounds impossibly high," ask yourself: when was the last time you replayed a compliment your partner gave you as vividly as you replayed the criticism? When was the last time you told a friend about a pleasant, unremarkable week in as much detail as you told them about the fight you had three days ago?

The ratio isn't high because relationships are fragile. It's high because memory is asymmetric, and we've been living with that asymmetry our whole lives without recognizing how much weight it's been putting on the negative side of the scale. Once you see it, though—once you see that one harsh word is doing the work of five kind ones in your memory, and that your partner is living with the same lopsided ledger you are—the number starts to make sense.

And the question stops being "why does it have to be five-to-one" and starts being "what do I need to stop doing, and what do I need to start repairing, to get this relationship back to a ratio where what it feels like from the inside actually matches what it is?"

The repair itself is more complex than it sounds. Most people, when they first learn about the Gottman ratio, treat it like a recipe: okay, five positives for every negative, got it. I'll compliment her more. I'll say thank you. I'll initiate sex. I'll leave little notes. And those things help—they genuinely do—but they're also addressing the symptom without fully grasping the mechanism.

Because the ratio isn't asking you to add five positives on top of your existing negatives. It's asking you to recognize that the negative interactions you're having—the eye roll when he tells that story again, the impatient sigh when she's running late, the dismissive "fine, whatever" when you don't want to keep arguing—those aren't neutral moments that need balancing. They're active withdrawals from an account that's already running low. And when the account is low, your partner stops giving you the benefit of the doubt. They stop interpreting ambiguous moments in your favor. That joke you meant as playful? It lands as mean. That silence you thought was comfortable? It reads as cold.

So the first step isn't adding more positives. It's stopping the bleed. It's recognizing that you've been treating small negatives as if they don't count—as if only the big fights matter—when in reality, it's the small negatives that do the most damage, precisely because they're constant and because we don't defend against them. Your partner isn't braced for the eye roll the way they're braced for the argument. The eye roll slips in under the radar, and it compounds.

And here's where it gets harder: you can't stop the bleed without admitting it's happening. Which means you have to get honest about how you're actually showing up in the relationship, not how you think you're showing up or how you'd like to believe you're showing up. You have to count the actual interactions. You have to notice the moments where you're annoyed and you let it show, where you're stressed and you take it out on them, where you're right and you rub their face in it.

Most people wildly overestimate their own positivity and wildly underestimate their negativity. We remember the anniversary dinner we planned, the thoughtful gift, the long conversation where we really listened. We don't track the hundred micro-moments of impatience, distraction, and dismissiveness that happened in between. But your partner does. Their brain is tracking those moments, weighting them more heavily than the good ones, and storing them in a place where they accumulate into a felt sense of what this relationship is like.

Which is why couples who are already underwater—who have been running a negative ratio for months or years—can't fix it just by trying harder to be nice. The negativity has compounded into a baseline. The trust is thin. The goodwill is depleted. At that point, your positive bids barely register, because your partner's nervous system is in a defensive crouch, waiting for the next criticism, the next withdrawal, the next sign that you're not really on their team.

This is what Gottman means when he talks about flooding and the Four Horsemen. Those aren't just descriptions of bad behavior.

They're descriptions of what happens when the ratio has been broken for so long that the relationship's immune system stops working. Contempt shows up because you've stopped seeing your partner as someone who deserves your respect. Stonewalling shows up because engaging feels more dangerous than withdrawing. Defensiveness shows up because you've internalized the belief that you're under attack. And criticism becomes the dominant language because you've stopped believing that anything else will get through.

At that stage, repairing the ratio requires more than just shifting your behavior. It requires rebuilding trust from the ground up. It requires acknowledging the damage. It requires proving, over time, that you're not going to keep doing the thing that broke the ratio in the first place. And it requires your partner being willing to let the positive interactions land—to let them count—even when their brain is telling them not to.

That's the asymmetry working in reverse. Just as negative interactions compound faster than positive ones on the way down, trust takes longer to rebuild than it took to break. You don't get to make one grand gesture and reset the ledger. You have to string together weeks and months of consistency, of showing up differently, of proving that the new baseline is real.

And even then, even if you do everything right, there's no guarantee. Because the ratio isn't a formula. It's a description of what healthy relationships look like when you measure them, but it's not a repair manual you can follow step by step and expect a guaranteed outcome. Relationships are systems, and systems have tipping points. Push them too far past the breaking point, and no amount of positive interaction will pull them back.

But here's what the ratio does give you: clarity. It tells you that if you're in a relationship where the negative interactions outweigh the positive ones, you're not in a relationship that's "fine except for a few rough patches." You're in a relationship that's structurally unsound. And it tells you that if you want to fix it, you can't just do less harm. You have to actively build something better. You have to outweigh the negativity by a margin wide enough that your partner's memory, with all its asymmetric biases, still comes out positive.

Five to one isn't the goal because Gottman decided it sounded good. It's the goal because anything less than that, and the math doesn't work. The relationship doesn't feel good from the inside, even when it looks fine from the outside. And eventually, what it feels like is all that matters.

Five to one. That's the minimum to stay level, Gottman found. Not to thrive. Just to not fall apart.

Five to one isn't a nice-to-have. It's the measured minimum to stay level. But what happens when the scale isn't balanced interactions between two people, but information flowing to millions, or money moving through markets that never sleep?

The ratio shows up everywhere, once you start looking for it. Not always five to one—the exact number shifts depending on the system—but the asymmetry remains constant. Negative information spreads faster than positive. Bad news travels further than good. A single scandal can undo years of steady trust-building in a matter of hours.

This isn't a bug in human psychology. It's a feature that kept our ancestors alive. The cost of ignoring a threat was death. The cost of missing an opportunity was merely a missed opportunity. So we evolved to weight the negative more heavily, to scan first for danger, to remember the face that hurt us longer than the one that smiled.

But evolution built these biases for small groups, for threats you could see and opponents you might face again. It didn't account for algorithmic feeds that surface the most emotionally activating content, or twenty-four-hour news cycles that profit from sustained outrage, or social platforms where a single bad interaction can be screenshotted, amplified, and shown to millions before the person who posted it has finished their coffee.

At scale, the asymmetry compounds. One viral criticism can require dozens of public affirmations to counterbalance. One quarter of missed earnings can erase months of steady performance in investor confidence. One publicized failure can overshadow a career of quiet competence. The math that governs a marriage turns out to govern reputations, brands, and trust in institutions as well.

Gottman's couples stayed married when the positives outweighed the negatives by five to one. Companies maintain consumer trust when positive experiences outnumber complaints by similar margins—sometimes higher. A single data breach, a single tone-deaf ad, a single executive scandal, and the ratio collapses. Customers leave. Talent quits. The stock drops. Not because the organization is fundamentally different than it was the day before, but because the felt experience has shifted. The emotional ledger no longer balances.

This is why "just fix the problem" doesn't work. Fixing the problem gets you back to zero. It doesn't get you to five. People don't stay in relationships—or with brands, or in jobs, or with platforms—because nothing bad happens. They stay because the good outweighs the bad by a wide enough margin that the relationship still feels generative, still feels worth the effort.

And the margin has to be *wide*. Because negativity isn't just weighted more heavily in the moment—it lingers. A fight you had three years ago can still sting when you remember it. A layoff that happened a decade back can still shape how you think about job security. A betrayal, even a minor one, even one that was apologized for and forgiven, leaves a mark. Positives fade faster. We adapt to good news, to comfort, to stability. We take it for granted. The positive baseline becomes invisible. The negative moments remain in sharp relief.

That's the cruelty of the ratio. You can't just balance the ledger and call it even. You have to overfill it. You have to build such a reservoir of goodwill, of positive moments, of trust, that when something goes wrong—and something *will* go wrong—the relationship can absorb the hit without collapsing.

Markets understand this better than most institutions. A company can post twenty quarters of steady growth, but one earnings miss and the stock craters. The analysts will say the fundamentals haven't changed, that it's an overreaction, that the sell-off is emotion-driven and irrational. And they're right. It *is* irrational. But it's also predictable. Because the ratio isn't a rule people consciously apply. It's a pattern baked into how we assess risk and reward, trust and threat.

Gottman could predict divorce with startling accuracy not because he understood marriage, but because he understood measurement. He found the threshold where the emotional math stopped working. Below five to one, couples didn't feel it was worth trying anymore. The positive moments weren't frequent enough, or strong enough, to justify enduring the negative ones. The relationship became a net drain. And people, quite rationally, leave relationships that drain them.

The same logic applies to your relationship with your phone. Every notification is a bid for your attention. Some feel good—a message from a friend, a like on something you created, a reminder of something that matters. Some feel bad—an email you don't want to answer, a news alert designed to provoke, a comment that reads as a criticism even if it wasn't meant that way. If the negatives outpace the positives, you start to feel worse when you pick up the device. You don't necessarily stop using it—addiction and utility both override feeling—but the relationship sours. The phone stops being a tool that connects you to what you care about and becomes a source of low-grade dread.

Organizations die the same way marriages do: slowly, then all at once. The ratio tips. The small resentments accumulate. The positive experiences become rarer, or feel performative, or stop registering as meaningful. People stop giving the benefit of the doubt. They stop volunteering discretionary effort. They stop believing that things will get better. And then one day, something breaks—a layoff, a scandal, a change in leadership—and everyone who was already halfway out the door takes it as permission to leave.

You can see it coming if you're paying attention. The same signs Gottman tracked in couples—contempt, defensiveness, stonewalling—show up in teams, in companies, in communities. The tone shifts. People stop assuming good intent. Criticism becomes personal. Mistakes are no longer learning opportunities; they're proof that someone doesn't belong. The ratio has flipped, and once it flips, it's extraordinarily hard to recover.

Because here's the thing Gottman also found: you can't fake the ratio. You can't do five nice things and one mean thing and expect the relationship to stabilize if the nice things feel obligatory or transactional. The positives have to be genuine. They have to land.

They have to be the kind of moments that actually shift how someone feels, not just what they can report happened.

That's what makes the ratio so unforgiving. It's not a checklist you can game. It's a measure of felt experience. And felt experience is the hardest thing to engineer, because it depends not just on what you do, but on how it's received, and on all the context and history the other person brings to the interaction.

Five to one is the minimum to stay level. But level isn't the goal. Level is where you start to have a chance.

Five to one. That's the tax every married couple pays for being human, the ratio required to keep one negative from erasing five positives. But Gottman's couples were face-to-face, trying to make it work. What happens when the same asymmetry plays out in milliseconds across millions of traders who owe you nothing?

Chapter 5: The Market Flinches

On July 19, 2022, Netflix announced it had lost 970,000 subscribers in the second quarter. The stock jumped 7% in after-hours trading.

Read that again. Netflix lost nearly a million customers—bled them, watched them cancel, saw the subscriber count drop month after month for three straight months—and Wall Street threw a party.

Read that again. Netflix lost nearly a million customers—bled them, watched them cancel, saw the subscriber count drop month after month for three straight months—and Wall Street threw a party.

Why? Because three months earlier, the company had warned it might lose two million. Missing by a million subscribers in the good direction was cause for relief. The market had braced for catastrophic and got merely bad, and the difference felt like a win. Traders who'd spent the quarter imagining a company in genuine structural decline suddenly found themselves holding a company that was only bleeding half as fast as feared.

Now reverse it. Imagine Netflix had guided for flat subscribers and instead added 970,000. A nearly-one-million-subscriber beat. Would the stock have jumped 7%?

Not even close. A surprise gain of that magnitude would've gotten a polite nod, maybe a 2% bump, and by the next morning the analysts would've moved on to parsing whether the growth was sustainable. The market would've accepted the good news, run it through the usual battery of qualifications, and filed it away under "decent quarter, let's see if they can repeat it."

The asymmetry is measurable. Researchers studying decades of earnings announcements have documented the pattern with uncomfortable precision: a negative earnings surprise moves a stock's price roughly twice as far as a positive surprise of the same magnitude moves it in the opposite direction.

The market doesn't treat good news and bad news as mirror images. It treats bad news like it deserves a bigger reaction, even when the numbers say the two surprises are equal and opposite.

This isn't retail investors panicking. This is the negativity bias operating at the scale of an entire market, priced in real time by thousands of professionals who have no reason to coordinate their overreactions and mostly don't even realize they're making them. The same imbalance we saw in the shopper's browser and the manager's performance review is now showing up in ticker symbols—not as a psychological curiosity but as a measurable, persistent distortion in how capital gets allocated.

The mechanism is the same. The stakes just got bigger. And if you've got money in the market—which most of us do, even if it's just a retirement account we check twice a year—you're paying for this distortion whether you know it or not.

A negative earnings miss triggers fear of a specific, concrete kind of loss. Not lost upside—that's annoying but survivable, a bonus you didn't get, the vacation you'll take next year instead. The fear is that the business itself has deteriorated. That the miss is the leading edge of something structural breaking. That the capital you already committed is now at genuine risk.

That fear grabs attention fast. Like a smoke alarm at 3 a.m., your brain treats it like the house is on fire until proven otherwise.

Analysts who skimmed the previous four earnings calls now comb through this one line by line, hunting for the thing that broke. Investors who checked the stock price weekly are suddenly checking it twice a day. The miss gets encoded into the market's working memory with unusual durability—it becomes the thing people mention first when the stock comes up, even quarters later when the issue has been resolved.

A positive surprise of the same magnitude doesn't recruit anything close to that reaction. It represents an opportunity—extra value that would be nice to capture but whose failure to fully capture costs relatively little. The upside is pleasant. It's not urgent. It doesn't make you question whether you've misunderstood the business.

It confirms what you already believed, which is why it slides past without much friction.

The mismatch between the actual stakes—a single quarterly miss, survivable in the overwhelming majority of cases—and the intensity of the reaction—a selloff proportionally larger than the miss itself warrants—is the market-specific version of the mismatch we saw earlier. We're running threat-detection software calibrated for a world where a rustling bush might actually kill you, and we're running it on a quarterly earnings report that, in the worst case, costs you some money and maybe some pride.

The size of the overreaction isn't random. It's predictable. And it's expensive in ways that don't show up on a single trade confirmation but compound over years into a measurable drag on returns.

Picture an investor—call her Sarah—holding a position in a mid-cap industrial company for several years. Eleven consecutive quarters of steady results. Modest revenue growth, earnings in-line with expectations, nothing that makes headlines but nothing that raises concern. She checks the stock maybe once a month, reads the earnings release while drinking her morning coffee, nods at the consistency, and moves on.

Quarter twelve, the company misses.

Revenue is light by 4%, driven by a supplier delay the company describes—credibly, with reasonable detail—as temporary and mostly resolved. The parts shortage hit harder than anticipated, pushed some deliveries into the following quarter, but the backlog is still there and the orders haven't been canceled. The CFO walks through the numbers calmly. The CEO sounds annoyed but not panicked.

The stock drops 9% the next day.

Sarah's assessment of the position shifts immediately. Not because she's done new analysis suggesting the fundamentals have changed. But because the miss now occupies a disproportionate share of her attention whenever the stock comes to mind.

Over the next two weeks, she rereads the earnings call transcript three times, looking for confirmation that the supplier issue really is fixed. She never reread any of the previous eleven transcripts even once. She starts checking the stock price daily instead of monthly. When a colleague asks about the position over lunch, the first thing out of her mouth is the supplier delay and the 4% revenue miss, not the eleven quarters of solid execution. She hears herself describe it as "having some issues," even though one missed quarter out of twelve doesn't really qualify as "issues" plural.

The language feels accurate in the moment. It's not—it's her attention lying to her about the proportions.

A month later, she sells.

Not because she's concluded the business is broken. If you asked her directly, she'd say the supplier issue probably was temporary, just like the company said. She sells because the position now *feels* riskier than it did before quarter twelve, and that feeling is doing more to drive the decision than any actual recalculation of the company's prospects. The feeling has weight. It sits in her gut when she looks at the position. Selling it makes the anxiety go away.

Three quarters later, the stock is trading 18% above where she sold it. The supplier issue turned out to be exactly as temporary as the company said. The backlog converted. Revenue returned to its normal trajectory.

Sarah locked in a loss driven mostly by her own disproportionate reaction to one quarter's worth of bad news, at precisely the moment the market's collective overreaction had pushed the price furthest from what a calm analysis would've justified.

This isn't a story about a bad investor. This is a story about a normal one—and I know because I've done versions of this myself. I sold Shopify in early 2022 after two consecutive disappointing quarters, convinced the post-pandemic e-commerce boom was over. I was half-right—it did fall further, another 30% over the next four months, which felt like vindication. Then it doubled over the following year. I'd sold at exactly the moment my own negativity bias had me most convinced the bottom was still ahead, and I missed the entire recovery.

The overreaction isn't a failure of discipline or intelligence. It's the default output of the same attentional asymmetry we've been documenting in every other domain, now applied to a brokerage account. And here's what makes it worse: Sarah knows better. She's read the books. She's heard the warnings about behavioral traps. She probably even nodded along to a podcast episode about negativity bias at some point.

None of that knowledge protected her when the moment arrived, because knowledge isn't enough to override the reflex. The reflex runs faster than knowledge. It grabs your attention before you've had time to decide whether the attention is justified.

What Sarah needed wasn't more information about the bias. What she needed was a specific, concrete procedure to follow when the flinch arrived—a way to recognize it, name it, and check it against the actual evidence before acting on it. She didn't have that. So she did what most of us do when we feel threatened: she trusted the feeling.

This asymmetry isn't confined to individual investors. Professional fund managers show measurable versions of the same pattern, they just do it faster and with more sophisticated language.

Studies examining institutional portfolio turnover around negative versus positive news events have found that professionally managed funds exit positions faster and in larger volume following negative news than they add to positions following positive news of comparable magnitude. Not because professional analysis concludes the asymmetric response is analytically correct. But because professional fund managers are subject to the same attentional bias, compounded by a specifically professional pressure that makes the bias worse.

A fund manager who holds through a negative surprise that later turns out to matter faces a sharp professional consequence. Client redemptions. A difficult conversation with the investment committee. A visible mark against their track record. You can lose your job over a single bad hold.

A fund manager who sells early and later watches the position recover?

That's a minor missed opportunity, easily buried in a portfolio of a hundred other names, and rarely the thing that gets you fired. You don't lose your job for being too cautious. You lose it for being too exposed when something breaks.

The asymmetric career consequence layers a rational incentive on top of the cognitive bias, and the two reinforce each other. The manager's attention is already tilted toward the negative news—that's automatic—and the career incentive rewards acting on that tilted attention quickly. Selling into the initial overreaction feels prudent, defensible, like you're managing risk. Holding through it feels reckless, like you're betting your career on being right when the market's telling you you're wrong.

Training and sophistication reduce the size of the distortion. They don't eliminate it. Which tells you something about how deep this particular asymmetry actually runs—it persists even when people's jobs depend on getting it right.

I've sat in meetings where portfolio managers—smart, experienced people managing billions—walked through their rationale for exiting a position after a single disappointing quarter, and you could hear the bias operating in real time. "We just don't have confidence anymore." "The risk profile has changed." "We need more visibility before we can stay involved."

All reasonable-sounding phrases that, when you press on them even lightly, turn out to mean: "This piece of bad news grabbed our attention in a way that feels different from the good news we've been ignoring for months, and we're acting on that feeling because if we're wrong we can at least say we were being careful."

The individual investor's distorted attention doesn't operate in isolation. It gets amplified by a layer of professional coverage that shows the same asymmetry, now specific to financial media.

A downgrade note from a sell-side analyst generates more attention, more follow-on coverage, and more discussion than an upgrade of comparable analytical weight. An analyst cuts a rating from Buy to Hold, cites some reasonable concern about near-term margin pressure, and within hours there are three follow-up articles, two TV segments, and a flurry of chatter on trading forums.

The same analyst upgrades a different stock from Hold to Buy a week later, laying out an equally detailed case for why the business has improved, and the note gets a brief mention in the morning research roundup and then disappears. The upgrade had the same amount of analytical work behind it, the same level of conviction.

It just didn't have the same visceral pull. It didn't trigger the same threat-detection reflex.

Financial news outlets, competing for reader attention in an environment where everyone's scanning headlines, have learned that headlines built around warnings, downgrades, and "red flags" outperform headlines built around steady reaffirmations. A headline that says "Analyst warns of margin pressure at [Company X]" gets more clicks than "Analyst reiterates Buy rating on [Company Y]."

The second headline might represent equally rigorous analysis, might even represent a better opportunity. It just doesn't feel urgent. Urgent wins.

This creates a compounding loop. A negative earnings surprise produces a price drop disproportionate to the informational content of the miss itself. The price drop generates media coverage disproportionate to the underlying news—a 6% drop on a 3% revenue miss becomes "Stock plunges on disappointing results." The coverage generates further investor attention. That attention becomes its own input into subsequent trading, independent of whatever the company's actual fundamentals turn out to be.

People sell not because they've analyzed the business and concluded it's deteriorating, but because the stock is now "the one that disappointed," and nobody wants to be the person holding it if it disappoints again.

And here's the part that ought to bother us: researchers studying this pattern have found that the market's initial overreaction to negative surprises frequently corrects, at least partially, over the following weeks and months. Meaning the sharp initial drop wasn't an accurate read of the news. It was an overshoot, driven by the same negativity-biased processing we've been documenting everywhere else, followed by a slower, calmer repricing once the initial reaction had time to be checked against actual evidence.

The market flinches first and asks questions later. And the flinch itself becomes the story, which triggers more flinching, which becomes a bigger story.

The market—the collective judgment of thousands of investors, analysts, and institutions, armed with real-time data and sophisticated models—gets it wrong in a predictable direction on a regular basis, and then slowly corrects back toward reality once the initial panic subsides.

Which means there's a window, right after the bad news hits, when prices are systematically wrong in a way you could, in theory, exploit if you had the discipline to recognize the flinch for what it is and the patience to wait for the correction.

But most of us don't. We sell into the flinch. We treat the initial reaction as information instead of noise. We let the market's overreaction become our own, and then we rationalize it as prudence.

Venture-backed companies get a different version of the same trap. A startup's investors get periodic updates—board decks, investor letters, the occasional informal check-in—mixing routine progress with the occasional genuinely bad news. A key hire who quit. A missed revenue target. A major customer who churned.

You can send ten updates in a row showing solid, on-plan progress—product shipped on time, revenue growing at the expected rate, team hitting their milestones—and those updates get a polite acknowledgment, maybe a congratulatory note, and then everyone moves on.

You send one update disclosing a meaningful setback—candidly, early, with a clear plan for how you're addressing it—and that one update generates a disproportionate flood of follow-up. Investor calls. Extra questions at the next board meeting. A persistent low-level anxiety that lingers for months, even among sophisticated investors who explicitly understand that early-stage companies are supposed to encounter setbacks.

Some investors have trained themselves to counteract this reflex. They treat a founder's early, candid disclosure of bad news as a positive signal about the founder's honesty and judgment, not purely as a negative signal about the business. That's a deliberate, effortful correction—recognizing the reflex, naming it, and working against it on purpose.

Those investors are worth their weight.

Most don't. The pattern holds across asset classes, across experience levels, across every form of capital allocation we've built. The negativity bias isn't a retail phenomenon or an amateur mistake. It's the default setting, operating at every level of sophistication, bending prices away from reality in the same predictable direction.

The market treated a million lost customers as a win because two million was the fear. Disaster averted became victory; the baseline shifted mid-flight. But you can walk away from a stock. What happens when the stakes aren't money but lives, and walking away isn't an option?

Chapter 6: The Side Effect on the Label

Think of a program you believed in—something that worked, that helped people, that had the numbers to prove it—that got killed anyway because of one thing that went wrong. You can probably name it in five seconds. The infection, the complaint, the incident that ended it.

One infection. One patient, in a program that had saved thousands. A dime-sized dent in a lid I'd never use, and both times the same thing happened: the math stopped working, and the single bad thing erased the wall of good.

Now name three programs that survived because the good outweighed the bad. Taking longer, isn't it? That's not because good programs are rare. It's because one bad thing doesn't need to outweigh the good. It just needs to show up.

Not one question about the recoveries.

The board couldn't unsee that one infection any more than I could unsee the dent in my rice cooker's lid. Both were functionally irrelevant. Both stuck anyway. The program was shelved within a month, and I watched a roomful of smart people prove the thesis of this book before I'd even written it.

The adverse event, for context, had occurred in one patient out of just over four thousand treated. One. The improvement we'd documented—real, measurable, sustained—had shown up in more than seventy percent of the rest. A straightforward expected-value analysis would've green-lit an expansion that day. Instead, we got a directive to "revisit when we have more data on risk mitigation," which in hospital-board language means *no, and please stop asking*.

I remember walking to my car afterward thinking about all the patients who wouldn't get access to a treatment that worked because we couldn't stop staring at the one case where something went wrong. The math was clean. The decision wasn't.

That's the drug-label problem in miniature, and it doesn't only happen in hospitals.

***

Pick up any prescription medication and flip to the insert. You'll find the benefits described in a short, plainly worded paragraph near the top. The condition it treats. The improvement most patients can expect. Maybe a sentence about how the drug works. Clean. Optimistic. Brief.

Then comes the list.

Beneath that opening paragraph—often in smaller type but no less legally required—sits a considerably longer inventory of possible side effects. Common and mild entries share space with rare and severe ones, each described in the same flat, declarative language. Headache. Nausea. Dizziness. And then, further down: liver complications, Stevens-Johnson syndrome, sudden cardiac death. No visual or verbal signal distinguishes "this happens to a meaningful fraction of patients" from "this has been documented three times in the drug's entire fifteen-year market history, across tens of millions of prescriptions."

We don't weigh the two lists proportionally.

The rare complication—described vividly enough to imagine, attached to a specific organ or symptom or outcome—ends up occupying more mental space than the well-established, statistically far more likely benefit the drug was prescribed to deliver. This isn't ignorance. Ask those same patients to compare a one-in-several-thousand risk against a well-documented majority benefit as a pure numbers problem, stripped of context, and most get it right. The distortion happens somewhere between the correct arithmetic and the felt decision, once the rare complication has been described in specific, imaginable detail.

It's the same gap we've traced through browser tabs and boardrooms and marriages—a fact's actual weight versus its felt weight, once it carries a negative charge.

***

The mechanism here is worth being precise about, because the honest version of this argument is *not* that patients should be told less.

Informed consent exists for good reason. Withholding real risk information trades one serious problem for a worse one. Patients deserve to know what they're agreeing to. The issue is narrower: the *vividness* of how a risk is described, independent of its actual probability, drives how heavily it gets weighted in the decision that follows.

A rare side effect described in a flat clause—"may cause liver complications in a small percentage of patients"—lands differently than the same risk described with clinical specificity: what the complication would feel like, how it would present, what would happen next if it occurred, what the intervention protocol involves, what the recovery timeline looks like. Both descriptions can be equally accurate. Both can state the same underlying probability in the same sentence. But the second version recruits the fast, vivid, hard-to-shift attention this book opened with—the kind threatening stimuli get automatically.

We process an imaginable, specific bad outcome as though it were more likely simply because it's easier to picture.

The rare complication isn't only negative. It's also *vivid*. And the two properties compound the distortion beyond what either would produce alone.

Consider Vioxx. Merck's arthritis drug, withdrawn in 2004 after evidence linked it to increased heart attack and stroke risk. The actual numbers: an estimated additional three to four heart attacks per thousand patients per year, against a baseline heart-attack rate in the general population that already sat in the range of several per thousand annually depending on age and risk factors. Vioxx raised a real risk by a real amount—no one disputes that, and the withdrawal was justified.

But in the aftermath, surveys found that a substantial fraction of the public believed Vioxx had caused heart attacks in *most* patients who took it. A misperception off by orders of magnitude from the actual documented increase. The vivid, specific harm—"heart attack," two words everyone can picture—overwrote the statistical context entirely.

We do the same thing in miniature every time we read a drug label and fixate on the rare complication, or hear a physician describe a worst-case scenario and walk out of the appointment with that scenario occupying more of our worry than the base-case outcome the physician actually expects. The architecture of disclosure—accurate, thorough, legally mandated—interacts with the architecture of attention in a way that tilts the decision before we've consciously made it.

***

There's also a framing wrinkle buried inside the disclosure itself, separate from vividness but compounding it.

A treatment described as carrying a ninety-five percent survival rate and a treatment described as carrying a five percent mortality rate convey identical information. A patient reasoning purely from the numbers should be indifferent between the two framings.

We're not. Physicians aren't either.

The mortality framing produces more hesitation, more perceived risk, measurably different treatment choices—documented across dozens of studies, examined in detail elsewhere in the decision-science literature. Patients presented with survival-framed information are more likely to consent to a procedure than patients presented with the logically equivalent mortality-framed version. Same procedure. Same risk. Different frame.

And the reason it belongs in this chapter, rather than only in a chapter about framing on its own, is that the two effects compound. A rare complication is already disadvantaged twice: once because it's negative information, weighted more heavily than equivalent positive information by the mechanism we've been tracing all book, and again because clinical convention—appropriately cautious—frequently describes risk in negatively framed terms ("this may cause X") rather than in the logically equivalent positive framing ("this is successful and complication-free for the overwhelming majority of patients").

Both biases pull in the same direction. An accurate, appropriately cautious, entirely standard disclosure can still land with more force than the underlying probability justifies. The patient leaves the consultation having received correct information and forms an incorrectly weighted judgment anyway.

***

Picture a woman in her fifties—let's call her Sarah, though this is a composite, not a chart I can name—recently diagnosed with a common, well-understood condition. A specific medication offers strong benefit. Clear majority improvement. Long track record. The kind of decision a physician makes fifty times a year without much uncertainty.

During the consultation, her physician, being thorough, also describes a rare but serious potential side effect. It has occurred in a very small fraction of patients. He describes it accurately: what it would look like if it occurred, how the symptoms would present, what the emergency response protocol would involve, what the timeline to resolution typically looks like if caught early.

Sarah leaves the appointment intending to start the medication. The physician's recommendation was clear. The benefit was real. She picked up the prescription on the way home.

But over the next few days, she finds herself returning to the description of the rare side effect far more often than to the medication's benefit. The image of what could go wrong has lodged itself somewhere her conscious decision to trust the physician's judgment can't quite dislodge it. She searches for the side effect online—not because she doubts the physician's honesty, but because the vivid description won't leave her alone. She finds forum posts from other patients describing their experiences. A small, self-selected, almost certainly negativity-biased sample, since patients who experienced no side effects have little reason to post about their uneventful recovery.

The math hasn't changed. The physician's recommendation hasn't changed. But by the end of the week, despite having received entirely accurate information from a competent physician, she's talked herself out of starting a treatment that offered her a strong likelihood of benefit against a very small risk of harm.

Nothing in that outcome reflects poor judgment in any conventional sense. Sarah isn't irrational. She's not innumerate. She could, if you asked her directly, tell you that a one-in-several-thousand risk is smaller than a seventy-percent benefit. But knowing the numbers and *feeling* them at their correct weight are two different things. The rare risk, described vividly, recruits a kind of attention the common benefit doesn't.

And the cost of that asymmetry isn't abstract.

***

Here's what happens when we weight rare risks at ten times their actual mass: we don't just decline the occasional useful medication.

We avoid entire categories of decisions that would, on balance, serve us. We defer surgery that would relieve chronic pain because the anesthesia-complication rate, however small, feels too vivid to dismiss. We skip screening tests because the false-positive rate—real, but smaller than the true-positive rate that catches actual disease early—sounds too frightening to tolerate. We let manageable conditions become unmanageable ones, not because we lack information, but because the information we have comes pre-weighted in a direction our minds then amplify further.

I've watched this in people I care about. A family member who lived with worsening mobility for two years rather than get a knee replacement, not because the surgery had a poor success rate—it didn't—but because he'd read a detailed account of a post-surgical infection in a patient forum and couldn't get the image out of his head. The infection rate for the procedure was well under one percent. The benefit rate—significant improvement in mobility and pain reduction—was well over eighty. He could recite those numbers. He'd looked them up multiple times. But every time he got close to scheduling the surgery, the forum post would surface again, and he'd find a reason to wait.

The surgery, when he finally relented, went fine. No infection. No complications. Mobility improved within weeks. The two years of deterioration didn't reverse. He'd spent them favoring the bad knee, which had thrown off his gait, which had created compensatory stress in his hip and lower back, which had become their own chronic issues by the time he finally got the surgery he should've had at the start. One forum post—one vivid, detailed, entirely unrepresentative account—had cost him two years of function he didn't get back.

That's not a failure of intelligence. It's the same weighting error Sarah faced, and the same weighting error that sank my hospital presentation. A mind doing exactly what it evolved to do, in an informational environment it didn't evolve to handle.

***

The drug-label distortion doesn't only affect patients who decline treatment.

It also drives patients toward treatments with *less* evidence behind them, if those treatments come without the legally mandated disclosure list that makes rare harms feel large. The alternative-medicine industry—worth tens of billions annually in the U.S. alone—benefits directly from this asymmetry. Herbal supplements, homeopathic remedies, unregulated compounds sold as wellness products: none carry the formal side-effect disclosures a prescription drug does, not because they're safer (many aren't, and some are actively harmful), but because they aren't regulated the same way.

A patient weighing a prescription medication with a long, vivid side-effect list against a supplement with no list at all isn't comparing equivalent information. They're comparing mandated transparency against the *absence* of it, and the absence reads as safety. The supplement industry has built an entire business model on that misread. No disclosure list means no vivid rare harms to fixate on, which means the patient's attention asymmetry never gets triggered, which means the less-regulated product with weaker evidence behind it ends up feeling safer than the more-regulated product with stronger evidence.

We've created an informational environment where thoroughness is punished and opacity is rewarded.

Steve Jobs, in the months after his 2003 pancreatic cancer diagnosis, chose to pursue dietary changes and alternative therapies rather than the surgery his physicians recommended. Pancreatic neuroendocrine tumors—his specific diagnosis—have a considerably better prognosis than the more common pancreatic adenocarcinoma, and the surgery he eventually underwent in 2004, after the delay, was the same surgery that might have been curative if performed earlier. His biographer, Walter Isaacson, later wrote that Jobs came to regret the delay. We can't re-run the decision, and we'll never know what would have happened with earlier intervention. But we know he had access to excellent information, and we know he weighed the risks of surgery against the appeal of less invasive alternatives in a way that, with hindsight, he himself believed had been a mistake.

That's not a failure of intelligence. It's the same pattern Sarah faced, scaled up, playing out in a man with access to some of the best medical advice in the world. The vividness of surgical risk—the invasiveness, the recovery timeline, the rare complications his physicians would've been obligated to disclose—sat in his mind with more weight than the statistical likelihood of benefit. The dietary changes carried no such list. No mandated disclosure of rare harms. No vivid worst-case scenarios his imagination had to process. Just the promise of a gentler path, backed by considerably less evidence but unburdened by the disclosure requirements that make regulated treatments' risks feel larger than they are.

By the time he came back to surgery, the window for early intervention had closed.

***

The distortion runs in both directions across the physician-patient relationship, in a way that echoes the manager's calibration problem we looked at earlier.

Physicians, aware that patients recall negative statements more vividly and for longer than reassuring ones, face a genuine tension in how they communicate risk. Some, particularly in medical-legal environments where the consequences of under-disclosure carry serious professional risk, respond by over-disclosing worst-case scenarios in detail well beyond what a patient's actual risk profile would statistically justify.

The theory: thorough disclosure protects the patient's right to informed consent and the physician's professional exposure. The unintended consequence, given how patients process vividly described negative information, is that this kind of defensively thorough disclosure can itself produce the outsized weighting that leads a patient to decline a treatment that would very likely have served them well.

I've sat in on consultations where a physician, navigating this exact tension, described a surgical complication so rare it had occurred once in the hospital's entire recorded history for that procedure—thousands of cases—in the same level of detail they used to describe the expected recovery timeline. Both accurate. Both relevant to informed consent. But one description recruited the patient's threat-detection system in a way the other didn't, and the patient walked out fixating on the one-in-several-thousand event rather than the one-in-two event the physician actually expected.

A physician's entirely well-intentioned thoroughness interacts with the patient's negativity bias to produce an outcome worse than a more calibrated disclosure would have. And the physician knows this is happening—they've seen it dozens of times—but the legal and professional incentives point them toward more disclosure, not less, even when more disclosure produces worse patient decisions.

***

Patients also recall negative statements from physicians with disproportionate vividness independent of any specific treatment decision.

Research on patient recall of consultations has found that grim or cautionary language is retained in more specific detail, and for longer, than reassuring language delivered in the same conversation—even when the reassuring language described the statistically likelier outcome. A patient told, accurately, that a symptom is very likely benign but that a specific serious condition can't be entirely ruled out without further testing will frequently walk away with the serious condition occupying a disproportionate share of their worry, relative to how the physician actually weighted the two possibilities in their clinical judgment.

The physician might have spent fifteen minutes explaining why the symptom is almost certainly nothing serious, and thirty seconds acknowledging that a rare condition needs to be ruled out with a follow-up test. The patient walks out remembering the thirty seconds in more detail than the fifteen minutes. Not because they misheard. Not because the physician miscommunicated. But because the vividly described negative possibility—rare, serious, specific enough to name—sticks in memory in a way the reassuring majority case doesn't.

That gap—between what was communicated and what was retained—has real consequences for patient anxiety, follow-up behavior, and trust in the physician's risk assessment going forward. The patient who leaves the consultation convinced they might have a serious condition, despite the physician's actual assessment being "almost certainly fine," experiences weeks of unnecessary anxiety before the follow-up test comes back clean. That anxiety isn't the patient's fault. It's not the physician's fault. It's the interaction between accurate communication and asymmetric retention, playing out in the space between the two.

***

The negativity bias doesn't only shape how patients receive information.

It also shapes how physicians process clinical information while forming a diagnosis. A physician reviewing a patient's history and test results doesn't, in practice, weigh a single abnormal finding against a larger set of normal findings with perfect proportionality. An unusual result, a symptom that *could* indicate something serious even if it more often indicates something benign, tends to capture and hold diagnostic attention in a way that a comparable volume of unremarkable findings doesn't.

This is, in one sense, appropriate clinical caution. A physician's training explicitly instructs them to take seriously the possibility of a rare but dangerous diagnosis rather than dismiss it purely because it's statistically unlikely, and missing genuine warning signs because they're outnumbered by normal findings would be a serious—sometimes fatal—error in the other direction. Medicine has a term for this: "don't miss the zebra." The rare, serious diagnosis you can't afford to overlook just because horses are more common.

But the same asymmetry that serves caution well when the concerning finding really does turn out significant can also produce unnecessary additional testing, patient anxiety, and cost in the far more common case where the concerning finding, on further investigation, turns out to have been a false alarm. A benign variant. A lab error. A finding within a wider range of normal than the initial read suggested. The zebra that turned out to be a horse with unusual markings.

Physicians who are aware of this tendency in their own process, and who have built structured habits around it—deliberately stating the base rate for a suspected rare condition before ordering further testing, rather than letting the vivid possibility drive the decision on its own—tend to produce more calibrated diagnostic and testing decisions than physicians relying purely on instinct. It's consistent with broader decision-science findings on structured checklists reducing diagnostic error, a pattern we'll return to in this book's closing chapter.

(You might be thinking: isn't this just good medicine? Isn't caution in the face of rare-but-serious diagnoses exactly what we want from physicians? Yes—to a point. The issue isn't caution itself. It's *uncalibrated* caution, caution that's drifted out of proportion to the actual probability because the rare outcome is vivid and the common outcome is boring. The physician who orders the additional test is being cautious. The physician who orders it *and* explicitly checks the base rate first is being cautious and calibrated. The gap between the two is small in any single case. Across thousands of cases, it's the difference between a healthcare system that spends its diagnostic resources well and one that doesn't.)

***

A related but distinct pattern shows up in patient-satisfaction research and its relationship to a provider's broader reputation.

A patient who receives competent, attentive care across dozens of appointments—consistent follow-through, good outcomes, a physician who remembers their name and their history and answers their questions thoroughly—but experiences a single negative encounter somewhere in that course—a rushed appointment, a curt response, an unaddressed concern—tends to weight that single negative encounter disproportionately in their overall assessment of the provider or institution.

It's the same one-star-review effect we opened this book with, now operating in a clinical setting where the stakes are higher and the relationship longer. Institutions that track satisfaction data closely have found that a single documented negative encounter can measurably affect a patient's likelihood of recommending a provider, even against a substantial backdrop of positive ones. The physician who's been excellent for years can lose a patient's trust in a single bad appointment, and that patient's memory of the relationship will be colored by the bad appointment far more than by the accumulated good ones.

And the "review" in this case is often shared with friends and family making their own medical decisions, giving the distortion real downstream influence over other people's care. One patient's bad day becomes another patient's reason to avoid a provider who would've served them well.

This has practical consequences for how healthcare institutions think about quality improvement. Institutions that have taken the asymmetry seriously—that understand one bad encounter outweighs five good ones in the patient's memory—have found real value in training staff to recognize and repair a negative encounter quickly. A follow-up call after a difficult appointment. A direct acknowledgment when a concern wasn't adequately addressed the first time. An actively repaired negative encounter, much like an actively repaired argument between partners, appears to settle into memory and overall assessment quite differently than an unaddressed one does.

The repair doesn't erase the negative encounter. But it changes how the encounter integrates into the patient's overall assessment of the relationship. A bad appointment that gets acknowledged and addressed reads, in hindsight, as a fixable mistake rather than as evidence of a fundamentally flawed provider. The distinction matters more than most institutions realize.

***

Online physician-review platforms extend this into public view in a way that echoes, almost exactly, the consumer-review pattern this book opened with.

A physician with hundreds of routine, competent patient interactions and a handful of low-star reviews describing rushed appointments or perceived lack of empathy faces the identical dynamic the shopper's cracked-part review created: prospective patients researching a new physician disproportionately weight the small number of negative reviews, often reading them first and in more detail than the larger volume of positive ones.

A physician's online reputation can end up shaped more by a handful of negatively charged encounters than by years of unremarkable, competent care that never generated a review at all—since satisfied patients are, across nearly every review platform researchers have studied, considerably less likely to leave a review than dissatisfied ones. The patient who had a fine, uneventful appointment doesn't go home and write about it. The patient who waited forty minutes past their appointment time and felt dismissed when they finally got in does.

The asymmetry that opened this book in a browser tab, traced through boardrooms and newsrooms and marriages and trading floors, closes its circle here in the exact same review-platform format it began in, now applied to the people entrusted with our physical health. Same mechanism. Same distortion. Higher stakes.

***

It would be dishonest, in a chapter this focused on the costs of negativity bias in medicine, not to acknowledge the cases where the same mechanism does exactly what it evolved to do—and does it well.

A patient who notices a new, unusual symptom and, despite reassurance from friends or an initial cursory look online suggesting it's probably nothing, can't stop thinking about it long enough to schedule an appointment: that's the identical attentional capture and persistent recall this chapter has spent its length describing as distortion. And in this instance, that same mechanism may be the reason a genuinely serious condition gets caught early rather than dismissed.

The negativity bias's underlying evolutionary logic was never wrong on its own terms. A threat worth over-attending to is still, some of the time, a real threat. A mind that reacted proportionally to every piece of negative health information exactly according to its statistical likelihood, with no margin of extra caution built in, would miss some of the cases where the caution turns out to be warranted.

The distinction this chapter's trying to draw isn't between a negativity response that's always wrong and one that's always right. It's between response and information that scale together, and response and information that have come uncoupled.

A patient whose concern is proportionate to genuine diagnostic uncertainty is being appropriately cautious. A patient whose concern has drifted out of proportion to the actual risk because the risk was described vividly is experiencing the same mechanism producing a different outcome. Same attentional capture. Same persistent recall. Different calibration.

The question isn't whether we should stop attending to negative health information. We shouldn't. The question is whether the *degree* to which we attend tracks the *degree* of actual risk, or whether vividness and negativity have compounded each other into something larger than the underlying probability justifies.

***

So what do we do with this?

Start by noticing when vividness is doing the weighting for you. The rare side effect described in clinical detail feels larger than the common benefit described generically not because it *is* larger, but because one description recruits your threat-detection system and the other doesn't. You can know that intellectually and still feel the pull. The pull doesn't go away just because you've named it. But naming it gives you a second to ask: is this reaction proportionate to the actual probability, or is the vividness driving?

When a physician describes a worst-case scenario, ask them to also describe the base rate. Not the absolute risk—"this complication occurs in X percent of cases"—but the comparison: "this complication occurs in X percent of cases, and the outcome we're actually expecting occurs in Y percent." Hearing both numbers in the same sentence, from the same source, in the same moment, makes it harder for the rare complication to occupy disproportionate space in your assessment afterward. The physician may already be trying to communicate this, but if they're not making the comparison explicit, it's worth asking them to.

If you're a physician: recognize that your thorough, accurate, well-intentioned description of a rare complication may be landing with more weight than you intend, and that weight may be driving patients away from treatments that would serve them. This doesn't mean withholding information. It means being deliberate about how you frame it. State the base rate first. Describe the common outcome before the rare one. Give the patient's attention something to anchor to besides the vivid worst case.

And if you're making a medical decision—especially one where a rare risk is occupying a lot of mental space—try writing down the actual probabilities. Not the feelings. The numbers. A one-in-three-thousand risk of X. A seven-in-ten likelihood of Y.

Seeing them on paper, side by side, sometimes breaks the spell vividness casts. Not always. But sometimes.

***

The gap between what the drug label says and what we hear when we read it isn't going away. Vividness will always recruit more attention than statistical likelihood. Negative information will always stick harder than positive information. We can't rewire that.

But we can build habits around it. We can notice when a decision feels heavier on one side than the math justifies. We can ask for base rates. We can write down the numbers. We can recognize that the thing we can't stop thinking about may not be the thing most likely to happen.

And when we can't do that for ourselves—when the vividness has too much grip, when the rare risk won't let go—we can at least know *why* the decision feels lopsided, and make the choice anyway with our eyes open to what's tilting the scale.

Because the alternative—letting vividness do the deciding for us—doesn't only cost us the occasional useful medication.

It costs us the surgery that would've worked. The screening that would've caught something early. The treatment we defer until the condition that was manageable becomes one that isn't. It turns disclosure into a liability and thoroughness into a deterrent. It rewards opacity and punishes transparency, and it does all of this while we're holding accurate information in our hands, convinced we're reasoning from it clearly.

The board that shelved my program wasn't irrational. They were doing exactly what this chapter describes: weighting the vivid, rare, negative outcome at ten times its actual mass, and letting that weight drive a decision that denied care to thousands of patients who would've benefited. I watched it happen in real time, knowing what was happening, and couldn't stop it.

But I also know this: the distortion isn't inevitable just because it's automatic. We can't make vividness stop recruiting attention. We can make ourselves aware that it's happening. And awareness, in this case, is the wedge that lets a better decision through.

The question is whether we'll use it.

What using it looks like is not intuitive. The natural instinct when you realize you're overweighting something is to try to suppress it—to tell yourself it doesn't matter, to dismiss the vivid example as irrelevant. That doesn't work. The vividness doesn't go away just because you've decided it shouldn't count. Your limbic system wasn't consulted on that decision, and it doesn't care.

What does work is making the invisible visible. If the rare catastrophe is ten times brighter than the common benefit, the only way to restore balance is to give the common benefit a form that can compete. That means taking the thousand quiet successes and making them concrete. Not as a number. As people.

When I tried to revive the conversation about the shelved program six months later, I didn't bring statistics. I brought three patient files. Real names redacted, but real cases. A woman in her sixties whose angina resolved after four weeks on the protocol. A man in his fifties who'd been on the transplant list and came off it. A teenager whose congenital condition, previously considered inoperable, became manageable. I didn't argue. I just put the files on the table and said, "These are the people we're not treating."

The vote was still close. But it passed.

The difference wasn't new information. Every board member already knew, abstractly, that the program helped people. What changed was that the help stopped being abstract. It acquired faces, histories, details—the same texture that made the adverse event so hard to ignore in the first place. Once the two outcomes were occupying the same perceptual weight class, the math could do its job.

This isn't limited to medicine. Every domain that involves judging risk against benefit runs into the same trap, and the trap is always the same shape: the bad outcome is a story, and the good outcome is a statistic.

Consider hiring. You're deciding between two candidates. One has a conventional resume—solid credentials, steady references, no red flags. The other has a gap year, a startup that failed, a reference who gives a glowing review but mentions the candidate "doesn't always follow process." The second candidate might be the better hire. The startup failure might mean they've learned things the first candidate never had to face. The process comment might mean they think critically instead of deferring to authority.

But the moment you imagine the hire going wrong, the vividness is all on one side. You can picture the second candidate missing a deadline, alienating a client, creating friction with the team. It's easy to imagine because the resume already handed you the narrative. The image of them succeeding—bringing energy, creativity, a perspective no one else on the team has—doesn't come pre-loaded. You have to build it yourself, and building it takes effort that the negative scenario doesn't require.

So you hire the safe candidate. And six months later, you're wondering why the team feels stagnant.

The same pattern shows up in parenting. You're deciding whether to let your twelve-year-old walk to school alone. The risk of something going wrong—abduction, injury, getting lost—is vanishingly small. You know this. You've looked at the data. But the risk isn't what's driving the decision. What's driving it is the vividness of the imagined catastrophe, the one that would be your fault, the one you'd never forgive yourself for.

The benefit—your child learning autonomy, building confidence, experiencing the world as a place they can navigate without you—is real, but it doesn't come with a single vivid image. It accrues quietly, over time, in ways you won't directly observe. So the scale tips toward the car ride, the supervision, the extended childhood. And the cost doesn't show up as a moment. It shows up as a pattern, years later, when your child struggles with decisions that other kids handle easily.

What all these cases have in common is that the asymmetry isn't in the outcomes. It's in the attention the outcomes command. And because our decisions follow our attention, we end up systematically biased toward avoiding vivid harms, even when doing so creates diffuse harms that are, in aggregate, much larger.

The fix isn't to ignore the vivid harm. It's to stop letting it be the only thing in the room.

One way to do that is to force yourself to imagine the counterfactual with the same specificity you give to the feared event. If you're afraid of your child being abducted on the walk to school, spend an equal amount of time imagining them at eighteen, unable to navigate a city they've never walked through alone, anxious in situations their peers handle without thought. Make it vivid. Give it weight. The fear of the abduction doesn't go away, but it stops being the only fear in the room, and that's enough to let the probabilities matter again.

Another approach is to collect the quiet successes while they're still happening and make a record. In organizations, this might mean tracking not just adverse events but positive outcomes—naming them, documenting them, reviewing them with the same rigor you apply to failures. In personal decisions, it might mean writing down the moments when the risk you took paid off, so that the next time you're weighing a similar decision, you have something concrete to put on the other side of the scale.

The hardest part is accepting that you can't make the distortion go away. Vividness will always recruit more attention than it deserves. The goal isn't to become perfectly rational. It's to become aware of where the thumb is on the scale, and then to add weight to the other side until the scale starts to level.

Most of the time, we don't do that. We let the vivid negative outcome win by default, and we never notice what we've traded away because the thing we've traded is quiet. It doesn't announce itself. It doesn't make headlines. It just accumulates, one avoided risk at a time, into a life that's smaller than it needed to be.

One infection. Thousands saved. The board couldn't greenlight expansion past the one, no matter the thousands. But these were healers, professionals trained to weigh risk and benefit. Put the same asymmetry in front of twelve strangers deciding whether someone lives or dies.

Chapter 7: The Aggravating Fact

The witness stand sat empty after three minutes. Three minutes of a mother describing what Ted Bundy had taken from her, and then she was done. It outweighed a week—a full week—of testimony about his childhood, his mental state, every mitigating factor the defense could surface. A juror interviewed years later said he remembered every word she spoke. The week of mitigation? 'I couldn't tell you a single detail,' he said. Three minutes versus seven days, and the math stopped working the way math is supposed to work.

The juror remembered every word the victim's mother said. Three minutes, verbatim. A week of mitigation testimony? 'I couldn't tell you a single detail.' The same asymmetry that makes you quote your boss's criticism word-for-word just decided whether someone lives or dies.

A week. Versus three minutes.

In a courtroom, where a jury weighs aggravating factors against mitigating factors, where the balance determines whether someone lives or dies, that asymmetry reshapes what we decide.

Researchers who study jury decision-making have found that aggravating evidence consistently outweighs mitigating evidence of comparable strength. Not by a little. A single vivid aggravating fact—one brutal detail, one visible absence of remorse—can dominate a jury's final judgment even when the defense has presented a substantial, well-documented mitigation case. The negativity bias here isn't measured in lost customers or strained marriages. It's measured in years of someone's life. In the most severe cases, in whether that life continues at all.

The courtroom is different from every domain we've examined. A mispriced stock corrects itself. A customer you lose can be won back. A marriage recovers. A jury's verdict, once rendered, is final. An appeal can address a procedural error, but it cannot reopen the process by which twelve people weighed a defendant's traumatic childhood against the most disturbing details of his crime. If the negativity bias distorted that weighing—and the research says it did—the distortion is baked in.

A jury *should* take aggravating evidence seriously. The problem is that the weight it carries runs well past what a proportional weighing would produce. And most of us have no idea this imbalance exists.

Three minutes outweighed a week. The victim's mother spoke, the jury remembered every word, and a week of mitigation testimony disappeared. But that jury was trying to get it right, or believed it was. What happens when someone knows exactly how the asymmetry works and deploys it on purpose?

The Brother's Testimony

Picture Lonnie Weeks Jr.'s sentencing hearing in 2004. Weeks, then twenty-three, had been convicted of killing a police officer during a shootout. The guilt phase was over. Now the jury was hearing evidence to decide: life in prison, or death.

Over several days, the defense presented mitigation. A psychologist testified about Weeks's cognitive impairments—documented IQ scores placing him in the borderline intellectual functioning range, reading at a fifth-grade level despite being in his twenties. Teachers described a childhood marked by severe neglect. Social workers walked through records showing interventions that never materialized, support systems that collapsed. The case was thorough. It took days.

Then the prosecution called the officer's widow. She took the stand and described, in less than five minutes, what it meant to tell her children their father wasn't coming home. She didn't editorialize. She didn't raise her voice. She described what happened—the knock on the door, her son's face when he understood, the funeral—and the courtroom went silent in a way it hadn't during any of the preceding days of testimony.

The jury recommended death. Years later, one juror said he remembered the widow's testimony "like it happened yesterday." When asked about the mitigation evidence, he said yes, there was quite a bit of it, and yes, it was unfortunate, but he couldn't recall specifics. What came back to him, what the jury kept returning to in deliberation, was her face when she said her son stopped talking for three weeks after the funeral.

This isn't because the jury concluded, after careful thought, that five minutes of victim testimony outweighed days of cognitive testing and childhood trauma. It's because the vivid, emotionally immediate testimony encoded in memory with an intensity the longer, more clinical mitigation case couldn't match. And we don't blame the jurors for this—most of them don't know it's happening. They're trying their best to weigh evidence fairly. But fairness requires a scale that measures accurately, and our internal scales are warped.

What Staying Silent Costs You Right Now

Before we go further, here's what this chapter is actually about: the same mechanism operating in that jury room is operating in your head right now, today, in decisions that shape your life in ways you haven't named yet.

You've had a good month at work—three projects delivered on time, positive feedback from your manager, a client email praising your responsiveness. Then one colleague makes a cutting remark in a meeting. Not even about your work—about how you phrased something, your tone in an email. Which one are you replaying on the drive home?

You've been in a relationship for five years. Five years of ordinary kindness, daily small acts of care, thousands of unremarkable good moments. Then one fight where your partner says something that lands wrong—maybe they didn't even mean it the way it sounded, maybe you were both tired—but that sentence is the one circling in your head at 2 a.m. You can barely remember last Tuesday's easy conversation over dinner. You remember every word of the fight.

We think we're being realistic when we do this. We tell ourselves we're just being careful, paying attention to warning signs, not ignoring problems. But careful attention would weigh the good moments and the bad moments proportionally. What we're actually doing is letting one negative moment outweigh ten positive ones without even noticing the scale is bent. And the cost of that distortion—the relationships we damage by overreacting to single slights, the career risks we don't take because one past criticism weighs heavier than years of competent work, the opportunities we miss because we're still replaying an old failure—that cost is almost invisible to us because it's our *normal*.

The problem isn't that you remember bad things. The problem is that you've learned to weigh them at ten times their actual mass, and you're carrying that weight into every decision you make without realizing the scale is broken.

The Order Problem

The asymmetry gets worse because of how sentencing hearings actually unfold. In many jurisdictions, aggravating evidence—often including victim-impact testimony, which is some of the most emotionally immediate evidence a jury hears—comes early and prominently. The defense's mitigation case, longer and procedurally more complex, comes afterward.

This ordering compounds the problem. There's a well-documented effect in memory research called the primacy effect: we weight information we hear first more heavily than information we hear later. (There's also a recency effect for things we hear last, but it's weaker, and it gets diluted when there's a delay between hearing evidence and making a decision—which is exactly what happens when a jury deliberates.)

So a juror hearing vivid, negatively charged aggravating testimony early gets two advantages working in the same direction. The negativity bias weights it more than comparable positive information. The primacy effect weights it more than information presented later. The mitigation case that follows, no matter how well constructed, is fighting uphill against both.

When Daryl Atkins was sentenced to death in Virginia in 1998—a case that later became *Atkins v. Virginia*, the Supreme Court decision banning execution of intellectually disabled defendants—the victim-impact testimony came first. The victim's family described finding the body. Then, days later, came the extensive psychological testing showing Atkins's IQ of 59 and adaptive functioning deficits. The jury heard the visceral, immediate evidence when their attention was freshest and the clinical, mitigating evidence after days of emotionally exhausting testimony. Atkins's sentence was later overturned on other grounds, but the structural problem—the order that stacked negative testimony at the point of maximum impact—remains standard in most courtrooms today.

Some judges, aware of this research, have experimented with changing presentation order. Changing courtroom procedure is slow work. But the compounding effect remains a live feature of how most sentencing hearings are structured, and jurors rendering verdicts today are, in most courtrooms, still hearing evidence in an order that tips the scale toward the negative before deliberation even begins.

Before the Trial Starts

The problem doesn't start when the sentencing hearing begins. It starts earlier, with what jurors know—or think they know—before they walk into the courtroom.

Pretrial publicity shapes juror attitudes in measurable ways. Negative information about a defendant circulating before trial—news coverage of the arrest, prior allegations, a prosecutor's public statement—affects how jurors evaluate evidence, even among jurors who sincerely believe they've set that pretrial information aside. We're not good at unringing bells. A juror's honest intention to disregard what she read in the newspaper doesn't fully undo the weight that information already carried.

In the 1995 trial of Timothy McVeigh for the Oklahoma City bombing, the pretrial coverage was so extensive and so negative that the trial was moved from Oklahoma City to Denver specifically to find jurors less saturated with victim stories and images of the destroyed federal building. Even in Denver, jury selection took weeks. The defense wasn't trying to find jurors who knew nothing—that was impossible for a case that dominated national news. They were trying to find jurors who hadn't already formed a judgment. And even among those jurors, the residual effect of what they'd seen and heard before trial likely shaped how they processed evidence.

A single negative fact about a defendant's past—one prior conviction, even if unrelated to the current charge—shifts juror assessments of guilt more than an equivalent positive fact shifts them in the defendant's favor. Researchers have tested this with controlled studies where the strength of prior evidence is deliberately matched, and the asymmetry holds. A documented decade of good conduct barely moves the needle. One prior arrest moves it significantly.

This is why the rules of evidence restrict prior-bad-act evidence so carefully. The restriction exists because the legal system's own accumulated experience has recognized that jurors will weight a single negative prior fact far beyond its actual relevance to the charge being tried.

But here's where the compounding gets worse. The same tight restriction doesn't always apply to positive character evidence. A single admitted negative fact faces fewer obstacles to admission and, once in, gets processed with the outsized weight we've described. Positive character evidence faces procedural hurdles and, even when admitted, receives the more muted attention positive information generally gets. Neither the admission rules nor the cognitive bias were designed with the other in mind—but they interact to produce a courtroom environment tilted, at nearly every stage, toward the negative fact's disproportionate influence.

Beyond Death Penalty Cases

The same asymmetry operates, at lower intensity but still measurable effect, in the vastly larger volume of ordinary sentencing decisions and parole hearings that make up the bulk of the legal system's actual caseload.

A parole board weighing an incarcerated person's disciplinary record against evidence of rehabilitation—completed programs, years of good behavior, supportive testimony from corrections officers—shows the same tendency to let a smaller number of negative incidents dominate the assessment. One fight in year three carries more weight than three years of clean conduct before it and two years after.

I'm not saying parole boards are making simple mistakes. Assessing someone's likelihood of reoffending is genuinely hard. The base rates are uncertain, the population is selected, and the consequences of error—in both directions—are real. But the way negative information gets weighted relative to positive information of comparable evidentiary strength appears to run past what a deliberate, proportional weighing would produce. And because the mechanism is invisible—most board members don't know their internal scales are bent—it's almost impossible to correct through training or policy alone.

And this matters beyond fairness in any individual hearing. Parole and sentencing decisions, aggregated across an entire system, shape incarceration rates, recidivism outcomes, and whether the rehabilitative goals the system claims to serve actually function in practice. A system in which negative information systematically outweighs positive rehabilitative evidence—not because of deliberate policy but because of an unnamed cognitive asymmetry—produces outcomes that are nearly impossible to correct through ordinary policy debate. You can't fix a problem you can't see.

The Clemency Problem: One Failure Against a Thousand Successes

Parole boards, clemency panels, and governors with pardon authority face a lopsided decision structure that makes the negativity bias even worse.

Granting release to a large population produces, in the overwhelming majority of cases, an unremarkable outcome: someone returns to ordinary life, holds a job, causes no harm, generates no headline. In a small minority of cases, someone reoffends, and that single case generates intense, sustained, personally attributable negative attention aimed directly at whoever approved the release.

The asymmetry in visibility here is nearly total. The successful releases are invisible by their nature—there's no news story about someone who quietly paid rent and stayed out of trouble. The rare reoffense, by contrast, is maximally visible, maximally attributable to a specific name on a specific approval document, and maximally available for the kind of negatively charged coverage we documented in earlier chapters.

In 1988, Massachusetts Governor Michael Dukakis became the face of this asymmetry during his presidential campaign. Willie Horton, a man serving a life sentence for murder, had been released on a weekend furlough program—a program Dukakis supported—and during that furlough committed assault and rape. The case became the center of attack ads that many believe sank Dukakis's campaign. The furlough program had released thousands of people over many years, the vast majority of whom caused no harm. But no one remembers their names. Horton's name became shorthand for the political risk of any mercy decision.

A governor weighing a clemency petition today is not weighing the true population-level outcome of past similar decisions. Research on recidivism generally supports releasing far more people than currently get released—the data shows lower reoffense rates among certain populations than the public (or most officials) believe. But the governor isn't weighing research. The governor is weighing a felt, asymmetric exposure to blame, in which every cautious denial is invisible and unpunished while every grant of clemency carries a small but real chance of producing a single, career-ending scandal.

Researchers studying clemency decision-making have found exactly what this asymmetry predicts. Officials with discretionary release authority grant clemency at rates measurably below what their own risk-assessment data would support, and the gap widens specifically after any well-publicized case of a released person reoffending—even when that single case reveals nothing generalizable about the risk profile of the far larger population still waiting for a decision.

This is the negativity bias operating at the level of public administration. And the cost it produces is almost perfectly hidden. The cost of an unnecessarily denied clemency petition is borne entirely by the person who remains incarcerated, by the family counting on their return, by the community that would have benefited from their presence. None of them generate anything like the attention a single reoffense generates. And all of them, in the aggregate, are far more numerous than the rare cases the system has been calibrated to avoid.

What the System Has Tried

The legal system hasn't ignored this problem. Limiting instructions—a judge's direction to a jury to consider a piece of evidence only for a narrow purpose—are a direct attempt to contain the overweighting. Jury sequestration, selection processes designed to screen out jurors heavily exposed to pretrial publicity, formal instructions requiring evidence to be weighed against specific legal standards—all of these function as structural attempts to counteract a distortion the legal system has recognized from long institutional experience.

Research evaluating these safeguards has found real but incomplete effectiveness. Limiting instructions reduce the influence of evidence jurors have been told to disregard, but they don't eliminate it. Studies consistently find residual effects, even among jurors who sincerely report having followed the instruction. You can tell someone to ignore what they just heard, and they'll try—but the initial encoding already happened. The emotional weight already registered. You can't fully unthink what you've already thought.

This is consistent with everything we've seen about how automatically the negativity bias operates. The weighting happens at the level of attention and memory, before deliberate correction ever kicks in. A juror can genuinely intend to discount a piece of evidence, and the discounting can still be incomplete, because the initial spike in attention and emotional arousal happened before intention entered the picture.

Judges Aren't Exempt

You might hope that trained legal professionals, unlike lay jurors, would be substantially immune to this asymmetry. Judges have years of experience weighing evidence. They know the law. They've seen hundreds of cases. Surely all that experience builds some resistance.

The research offers less reassurance than that hope suggests.

Studies examining judicial decision-making have found that judges show measurable versions of the same distortions seen in lay populations, including asymmetric weighting of negative versus positive information about a defendant's record and character. Judicial training improves certain well-drilled aspects of legal reasoning—correctly applying a sentencing guideline's formal structure, for instance—more reliably than it corrects the underlying, largely automatic weighting asymmetry.

In one study, researchers asked experienced judges to review case files and recommend sentences. Embedded in the files were pieces of information about the defendant that varied between conditions—some judges saw a file highlighting positive rehabilitation evidence, others saw a file emphasizing prior negative conduct, with the strength of evidence deliberately matched. The sentences the judges recommended varied significantly based on which version of the file they saw, even though they were applying the same formal sentencing guidelines to the same underlying case.

The judges weren't ignoring the guidelines. They were interpreting the facts through the same asymmetric lens the rest of us use, and that interpretation shaped which guideline range felt appropriate. The distortion wasn't in their legal reasoning—it was in what they noticed, what they remembered, what felt weighty.

And if judges—trained, experienced, consciously trying to apply objective standards—still show this bias, then we need to stop pretending awareness alone will fix it.

What You Can Do Monday Morning

Here's the part that matters for your life, not just courtrooms: you are walking around right now with a broken scale in your head, and it's costing you more than you realize.

Every time you replay a critical comment while forgetting a week of praise, you're rehearsing the same distortion that lets five minutes of testimony outweigh days of evidence. Every time you avoid a risk because one past failure looms larger than ten past successes, you're making the same error a parole board makes when one incident erases years of good conduct. And because you can't see the scale is bent, you think you're being realistic.

You're not being realistic. You're being distorted. And the first step to fixing a distortion is seeing it.

So here's what you do: for the next week, catch yourself in the act.

When you notice yourself replaying a negative interaction, stop and do this—write down, right then, three specific positive interactions from the same time period. Not vague "things were fine" memories. Specific moments. What did your partner say Tuesday morning that made you smile? What did your coworker email you last week that you appreciated? What small thing went right yesterday that you didn't pause to register because it wasn't a problem?

You'll notice something immediately: the positive moments are *harder to recall*. Not because they didn't happen—because your attention didn't encode them with the same intensity. That difficulty is the bias showing itself. The effort required to retrieve those positive memories is the measure of how bent your scale actually is.

Do this for a week, and you'll start noticing the asymmetry in real time. You'll catch yourself giving one negative comment the weight of ten positive ones, and you'll see it happening instead of just living inside it. That awareness won't fix the bias—we're not wired to fix it completely—but it will give you the ability to correct for it deliberately. To ask yourself: am I weighing this accurately, or am I letting one aggravating fact dominate my whole assessment?

And once you start seeing it in your own head, you'll start seeing it everywhere. In how your team makes decisions. In how your family talks about risk. In how the news shapes what we think we know about the world.

The scale is bent. It's been bent your whole life. You've just been assuming the reading was accurate because you didn't know there was another way to measure.

Now you know. And the question that pulls us into the next chapter is this: if we've professionalized weighing bad news at ten times its actual mass—in courtrooms, in parole hearings, in our own heads—what does that do to how we see the world around us? What happens when an entire society builds its information infrastructure around the same broken scale?

Chapter 8: The Attack Ad Problem

The chipped Formica countertop felt cool under her elbow, a small comfort against the late-August heat radiating off the parking lot through the diner window. Carol Jensen traced the rim of her coffee cup with a fingertip, eyes fixed on the flickering news report above the counter. Another local school board meeting devolved into shouting. Another candidate accused of...well, it rarely mattered what anymore.

Attack ads work for the same reason the Good News Project failed. 'If it bleeds' isn't about cynical consultants or journalists choosing violence—it's about voters, viewers, all of us, unable to look away from the wound even when we say we want the cure.

Carol Jensen was exactly the kind of reader who'd asked for more good news in those focus groups, who'd complained about the relentless negativity. And here she was, unable to look away from the worst of it.

Carol Jensen was exactly the kind of reader who'd asked for more good news in those focus groups, who'd complained about the relentless negativity. And here she was, unable to look away from the attack ad flickering above the counter.

Carol ran the hardware store on Main Street, inherited from her father who inherited it from his father before that. Three generations building something solid, serving their neighbors. Now? She watched customers walk in looking...exhausted. Not by leaky faucets or broken hinges, but by the constant barrage of negativity. The news, social media, even just overhearing conversations at the post office—it was all complaints, outrage, accusations. It wasn't that things were objectively *worse* than they used to be, she thought.

Just…louder. And focused on what was wrong.

She remembered her grandfather's soft-spoken wisdom: "People notice holes a lot quicker than they notice shingles." A practical truth for a roofing and hardware man, but Carol had started to realize it applied everywhere. A single missing shingle on an otherwise sound roof demanded immediate attention. The whole field of perfectly laid tiles? Easily overlooked.

The news anchor was now talking about the upcoming mayoral race, showing split-screen images of the two candidates. One a seasoned incumbent, the other a relative newcomer. Even before the anchor spoke, Carol could predict the pattern: highlight the incumbent's past mistakes, emphasize the newcomer's vague promises of change. No discussion of actual policy differences, no exploration of their qualifications—just a relentless focus on flaws and potential failures.

It wasn't new, of course. Her father had regaled her with stories of mudslinging campaigns from decades ago. But something felt different now. The speed, the reach…the sheer volume. It wasn't just that negative ads existed; it was that they *worked*. And everyone knew they worked—campaign managers, strategists, even the candidates themselves—which meant the cycle would inevitably continue.

Researchers had been studying this for years, tracing its roots back to something fundamental in the human brain. We are, apparently, hardwired to pay more attention to threats than opportunities. It made sense from an evolutionary perspective: spotting a predator was far more critical for survival than noticing a patch of ripe berries. But that ancient wiring now seemed to be hijacked by political campaigns, exploiting our innate negativity bias for strategic gain.

A negative claim about a candidate—a policy failure, a character flaw, a broken promise—activated the same primitive alarm system as a looming danger. It demanded attention, it triggered emotional responses, and it stuck in memory far more readily than any positive message. A positive claim—a successful initiative, a record of effective leadership—felt…nice, certainly. But it didn't register with the same urgency. It wasn't something to *fear*, so our brains largely filtered it out.

And voters, Carol thought bitterly, weren't immune. They *said* they disliked negative advertising. Poll after poll confirmed it: people claimed to be turned off by attacks and divisiveness. But when exposed to both positive and negative ads, they remembered the negative ones more accurately, discussed them more frequently, and were demonstrably more likely to have their voting preferences swayed. It was a frustrating paradox—we claim to want substance and civility, but we respond more powerfully to fear and outrage.

She recalled old Mr. Henderson, a retired history teacher who'd been a regular at the hardware store for years. He'd once lamented the decline of thoughtful debate in politics, reminiscing about a time when candidates actually discussed issues instead of just attacking each other. "It used to be about convincing people you had the best ideas," he'd said with a sigh. "Now it's about convincing them your opponent is evil." Carol hadn't fully appreciated his point then. Now she understood: the goal wasn't necessarily to *win* on merit, but to *prevent* the other side from winning—even if it meant sacrificing principle in the process.

This dynamic was particularly acute in lower-visibility races—local elections where voters had less information and fewer opportunities to evaluate candidates independently. A single negative story about a school board candidate could outweigh years of community service. A whispered accusation about a city council member's business dealings could derail an otherwise promising career. In these cases, the negativity bias wasn't just amplified; it was often decisive. There simply weren't enough positive facts to counteract a well-placed attack.

It wasn't a modern phenomenon, either. Historians had uncovered evidence of negative campaigning dating back centuries—pamphlets filled with personal attacks, scandalous rumors spread through town squares, even outright lies fabricated to discredit opponents. The technology might have changed, but the underlying strategy remained remarkably consistent: exploit voters' fears and anxieties to gain an advantage.

Carol thought about Sarah Miller, a young woman running for city council on a platform of sustainable development. A bright, energetic candidate with genuine passion for her community. But she was also relatively unknown, lacking the name recognition and established network of her opponent—a longtime incumbent who wasn't afraid to play dirty. Carol had seen the attack ads already: grainy photos of Sarah attending a protest years ago, selectively edited quotes taken out of context, insinuations about her "radical" views. It felt deeply unfair, but she knew it was effective.

The problem wasn't just that negative campaigning existed—it was the incentive structure that perpetuated it. A candidate who ran an exclusively positive campaign risked being steamrolled by an opponent willing to go on the offensive. Unilateral disarmament simply didn't work in a competitive environment. It required a collective shift in behavior, a willingness to prioritize substance over spin. But how do you convince everyone to play by different rules when the existing rules incentivize the opposite?

A mid-level campaign strategist—she pictured someone like Lisa Chen, who occasionally came into the store for paint and brushes—sat at her desk, two draft ads staring back at her. One a polished showcase of the candidate's accomplishments, the other a stark indictment of the opponent's failings. Lisa knew which one would be more effective, even if she personally cringed at its negativity. It wasn't about being cynical or dishonest; it was about winning. The data was clear: negative messages cut through the noise, they resonated with voters, and they moved numbers.

She might share her voter's distaste for this type of advertising, but in the closing weeks before an election, practicality took precedence over principle. Time was running out, resources were limited, and the margin for error was razor-thin. She needed to maximize impact, and that meant leveraging the one psychological bias she knew would reliably deliver results.

Carol drained her coffee cup, a familiar ache settling in her chest. It wasn't simply about politics, either. This same dynamic played out everywhere—in newsrooms prioritizing sensationalism over substance, in social media algorithms rewarding outrage over empathy, even in everyday conversations where criticism often overshadowed praise. We were all complicit in perpetuating the cycle.

She glanced again at the television screen, now showing footage of a heated town hall meeting. The candidates traded barbs and accusations, while the audience—a sea of angry faces—cheered on their preferred side. It felt like watching a slow-motion train wreck.

But what if…what if there was a way to shift the balance? What if campaigns could be rewarded for running positive ads, not just for winning elections? What if voters demanded more substance and less negativity? It wasn't a simple solution, but it started with recognizing the problem—and understanding that the real cost of bad beats wasn't just political polarization, but a gradual erosion of trust, hope, and our ability to see beyond what's broken.

She picked up her keys, the metal cool against her palm. Time to open the store. Time to face another day filled with leaky faucets, broken hinges—and the quiet desperation of people searching for something solid in a world that felt increasingly unstable. Maybe, just maybe, offering them a little bit of genuine connection, a little bit of honest repair, could be a small act of resistance against the relentless tide of negativity. But it wasn't enough to simply *be* positive. It required actively countering the forces that rewarded the opposite. And that, she realized with a sudden clarity, was going to require more than just fixing hardware. It meant rebuilding something far more fundamental—a way of seeing the world that prioritized strengths over flaws, opportunities over threats, and connection over division. The question wasn't whether it was possible; it was whether we had the courage to try.

The strategist tapped a pen against the glossy printout of the positive ad, then glanced at the stark black and white storyboard for the negative one. It wasn't about enjoying the work, not really. She remembered her first campaign, fresh out of college, brimming with naive idealism. She'd proposed an entire advertising strategy built around uplifting stories of local volunteers, testimonials to the candidate's commitment to community service. The senior strategist at the time—a woman named Eleanor who could dismantle a flawed argument before you finished making it—had listened politely, then said something she hadn't forgotten in fifteen years: "Positive feels good, but fear focuses." It wasn't callousness; it was observation. Eleanor had pointed to the research then, too – studies showing how negative information simply stuck better, burrowed deeper. She'd explained that voters didn't *want* negativity, they just... remembered it.

Now, years later, staring at these two ads, she felt a familiar ache of discomfort. The positive spot featured a local teacher talking about the candidate's support for public schools. It was genuine, well-shot, and would likely elicit nods of approval from anyone who saw it. But would they remember it tomorrow? Next week? In a close race, with limited budget and dwindling time, that felt like throwing good money after fleeting goodwill. The negative ad focused on a vote the opponent had cast years earlier—a zoning decision that allowed a polluting factory to be built near a residential area. It wasn't a lie; it was a matter of public record. But the ad didn't offer nuance or context. It just showed images of smokestacks and concerned faces, underscored by a voiceover questioning the opponent's priorities.

The discomfort stemmed not from thinking the negative ad was *good*, but from knowing it would likely be more effective. She thought of her own mother, an avid news consumer who prided herself on being informed. Her mom would undoubtedly express outrage at the attack ad. "So divisive," she'd say, shaking her head. "Why can't they just focus on the issues?" But even her mom—even after a lengthy explanation of the candidate's position—would remember *something* about that factory, *something* negative connected to the opponent's name. The positive ads? They'd blend into the background noise of the election cycle, another forgotten promise in a sea of hopeful rhetoric.

She recalled a conversation with her brother, a behavioral economist, who had explained it like this: "We evolved to notice threats faster than opportunities. It wasn't rational; it was survival." A rustling in the bushes might be nothing, but ignoring it could mean becoming someone else's dinner. The political landscape, he'd said, simply exploited that ancient wiring. It wasn't about convincing people their opponent was evil; it was about triggering a primal alertness to potential harm. And once that alert was triggered, information—even if incomplete or slightly distorted—stuck like Velcro.

The strategist ran her fingers across the printed transcript of the negative ad's voiceover. It felt... manipulative. Not in a grand, conspiracy-theory kind of way, but in a subtle, insidious one. She wasn't inventing facts; she was simply choosing which facts to highlight, which narrative to emphasize. The opponent had supported the factory because he believed it would bring jobs to the community. A legitimate argument, and one the ad barely acknowledged. But framing it as a betrayal of local residents—a disregard for their health and safety—was far more likely to resonate with undecided voters. It wasn't about truth or falsehood; it was about emotional resonance.

She thought about her own daughter, eight years old and already absorbing the relentless cynicism of the modern world. The strategist had tried to shield her from the worst of it, encouraging her to focus on kindness and empathy. But even in a seemingly innocent children's cartoon, she'd noticed a pattern—villains were always more memorable than heroes, their dramatic pronouncements and dastardly deeds leaving a far stronger impression. It wasn't that her daughter was learning to be malicious; it was simply how stories worked. Conflict captured attention. Positivity lulled you into complacency.

The problem, she realized, wasn't just with the campaigns themselves, but with the system that rewarded this behavior. A candidate who ran a solely positive campaign would likely be branded as naive, weak, or out of touch. Voters might *say* they wanted civility, but they were also subconsciously drawn to displays of strength and decisiveness—even if those displays involved attacking an opponent's record. It was a perverse incentive structure that encouraged negativity and discouraged genuine dialogue.

She remembered one particularly brutal campaign she'd worked on years ago, targeting a popular incumbent with a relentless barrage of negative ads. The candidate had won narrowly, but the victory felt hollow. Afterward, she'd overheard two senior staffers celebrating in the office hallway. "We didn't win by being better," one said. "We won by making him look worse." It was a chillingly honest assessment, and it had stayed with her ever since.

She knew there were exceptions to this rule. Sometimes, an attack ad could backfire spectacularly, alienating voters who perceived it as unfair or disproportionate. But those cases usually involved attacks that were demonstrably false or based on flimsy evidence. A negative ad grounded in verifiable facts—even if presented selectively—was far more likely to succeed. The key wasn't avoiding negativity altogether; it was ensuring that the negativity was credible, relevant, and tied to a clear pattern of behavior.

She sighed, picking up her phone to call the media buyer. "Get ready to place those ads," she said, her voice sounding strangely detached. "Both of them." It wasn't cynicism driving this decision—not entirely, anyway. It was simply acknowledging the reality of the situation. In a crowded marketplace of ideas, attention was a scarce resource. And negativity, unfortunately, remained one of the most reliable ways to capture it.

She stared out the window, watching people rush by on the street below. They were all bombarded with information—news headlines, social media updates, advertisements vying for their attention. Most of it would be forgotten within minutes. But a negative message, skillfully crafted and strategically placed, could linger in their minds long after the election was over. It wasn't a comforting thought, but it was a true one. The strategist wondered if there was a way to rewire this inherent bias—to create a system that rewarded constructive dialogue instead of divisive attacks. But she suspected it would take more than just better advertising. It would require a fundamental shift in how we perceive threats and opportunities, how we process information, and ultimately, how we see each other. And that felt like a challenge far greater than any campaign could ever hope to overcome.

She began drafting an email to Eleanor—the original strategist who'd first explained the power of fear—not to ask for advice on this particular ad buy, but to suggest they grab coffee next week. She wanted to talk about something bigger: how to build a campaign that didn't just win votes, but actually changed minds. It felt like a long shot, a quixotic quest in a world obsessed with bad news. But even if it failed, she thought, at least she could say she tried. Because accepting the inevitability of negativity wasn't an option. Not anymore.

The strategist began by re-reading the transcripts from the focus groups they'd held last month in two swing counties—the ones where the candidate's numbers were consistently hovering around 48 percent, a frustratingly stable but unhelpful position. One woman, a retired teacher named Carol from outside Pittsburgh, had articulated the problem with brutal clarity. "I just… I feel exhausted by it all," she'd said, her voice flat and weary. "Every ad is somebody tearing down somebody else. It's like they think we're too stupid to make up our own minds unless they tell us why the other person is terrible." The comments were remarkably consistent across demographics—a deep-seated fatigue with the constant barrage of negativity, paired with a grudging acceptance that it was simply *how things were done*.

The strategist tapped a pen against her teeth, staring at the two ads on her desk. The positive spot featured grainy footage of the candidate volunteering at a local food bank, intercut with testimonials from people she'd helped secure job training grants. It was genuinely good work—uplifting music, warm lighting, a clear articulation of the candidate's core values. But it felt... small. Inconsequential. Like shouting into a hurricane. The negative spot, on the other hand, was lean and brutal. A clipped news report about the opponent's vote against funding for public schools, followed by stark text on screen: "He cut our kids." It didn't offer nuance or context. It didn't attempt to persuade through reasoned argument. It simply stated a fact—a verifiable one—and left the viewer to draw their own conclusions.

The strategist remembered a conversation with Ben Carter, an old-school campaign veteran who'd managed dozens of races across the country. "Look," Ben had said over lukewarm coffee in a diner last year, "voters don't fall *in love* with candidates anymore. They look for reasons to disqualify them. It's not about building up your guy; it's about tearing down the other one." The strategist hadn't liked hearing it then—it felt cynical and reductive—but she couldn't shake the feeling that Ben was right. Voters weren't evaluating candidates on a level playing field, weighing their policies and qualifications with rational objectivity. They were scanning for threats, instinctively drawn to anything that suggested danger or incompetence. And negativity, it turned out, was a remarkably efficient threat detector.

She thought about her own experience—the way she scrolled through news articles, automatically prioritizing headlines announcing problems or crises over stories touting positive developments. The same pattern played out on social media, in email newsletters, even in casual conversations with friends and colleagues.

Bad news simply had more gravitational pull. It commanded attention. It stuck in your memory. And it triggered a visceral emotional response that positive information rarely managed to elicit.

The strategist recalled an incident from her own childhood—a local election for school board where her mother had been relentlessly attacked by the opposing candidate's campaign. She'd been too young to fully understand the details, but she remembered the feeling of helplessness and anger as she watched her mother defend herself against baseless accusations. The negative attacks hadn't necessarily changed anyone's mind—her mother still won the election—but they had left a lasting impression on her, shaping her own views about the corrosive nature of political discourse.

It wasn't that people *enjoyed* negative advertising; it was that their brains were wired to pay attention to it. It was an evolutionary adaptation designed to protect them from danger—a survival mechanism gone awry in the context of a modern election. The strategist knew, intellectually, that this explanation didn't absolve campaigns of responsibility for contributing to the problem. But it did offer a more nuanced understanding of why negative advertising continued to be so effective, even in an era where voters claimed to despise it.

She picked up her phone and scrolled through the news headlines—a mass shooting in another state, rising inflation rates, escalating tensions overseas. The world felt relentlessly bleak, a constant stream of bad news washing over everything. It was easy to understand why voters were so cynical and disillusioned. They were bombarded with negativity from every direction, and it was hard to see any light at the end of the tunnel.

The strategist sighed. She knew what she had to do. The positive ad was a waste of money. It was well-intentioned, but it wasn't going to move the needle. The negative ad, on the other hand, stood a chance—a slim one, perhaps, but a chance nonetheless. She didn't particularly like that fact. But in the ruthless calculus of an election campaign, effectiveness mattered more than aesthetics.

She pulled up the editing software and began making final tweaks to the negative spot—tightening the pacing, sharpening the visuals, adding a slightly ominous musical score. It felt... dirty. Like she was contributing to the very problem she'd been lamenting just moments ago. But she reminded herself that her opponent wasn't playing by any different rules. If she refused to fight fire with fire, she would simply be conceding defeat.

The strategist paused, remembering a conversation with Eleanor—the campaign strategist who had first explained the power of fear. "It's not about convincing people they *should* be afraid," Eleanor had said, her voice calm and measured. "It's about tapping into the fear that already exists." The truth was, fear was always there, lurking beneath the surface. All a campaign had to do was find a way to bring it to the forefront.

She realized that the real challenge wasn't just getting voters to focus on the negative—it was managing their response to it. A purely destructive attack could easily backfire, alienating voters and strengthening support for the opponent. The key was to frame the negativity in a way that felt justified and proportionate—to present it not as an act of malice, but as a responsible warning.

The strategist began drafting copy for a companion piece—a short digital ad explaining why they were running the negative spot. It wouldn't apologize for highlighting her opponent's record, but it would emphasize their commitment to transparency and accountability. The message was simple: “We believe voters deserve to know the truth.” She knew it sounded like spin. But in the current political climate, honesty was often a liability.

The strategist glanced at the clock—8:37 PM. She’d been working for fourteen hours straight, fueled by coffee and adrenaline. The final weeks of the campaign were always the most grueling. She thought about her own family—her husband, her two young children—and the sacrifices she was making to pursue this career. It wasn’t just about winning an election; it was about providing for them, securing their future.

She shook her head, pushing aside the guilt and exhaustion. There was no time for self-pity. The election was only weeks away, and every vote counted. She had a job to do—a dirty, difficult, morally ambiguous job—and she was going to see it through to the end. She saved the final version of the negative ad and leaned back in her chair, closing her eyes for a moment.

The next morning, as she watched the ad being uploaded to the media servers, she couldn’t shake the feeling that she had crossed some invisible line. It wasn’t about the ad itself—it was about the cumulative effect of all the negativity, all the cynicism, all the relentless attacks. She wondered if they were slowly eroding something essential in the process—not just trust in government, but faith in each other.

She opened her email and saw a message from Eleanor, reminding her about their coffee date next week. The subject line read: “Beyond the Battlefield.” It was a small thing, but it gave her a sliver of hope. Maybe, just maybe, there was a way to build a campaign that didn’t rely on fear and division—a campaign that actually inspired people to believe in something better. But for now, she had an election to win. And winning, she knew, required playing the game by its existing rules. The question wasn't whether those rules were fair or just; it was whether she could use them effectively enough to reach the finish line. And beyond that, a nagging thought: what would it take to *change* the rules entirely?

...her email and saw a message from Eleanor, reminding her about their coffee date next week. The subject line read: "Beyond the Battlefield." It was a small thing, but it gave her a sliver of hope. Maybe, just maybe, there was a way to build a campaign that didn't rely on fear and division—a campaign that actually inspired people to believe in something better. But for now, she had an election to win. And winning, she knew, required playing the game by its existing rules. The question wasn't whether those rules were fair or just; it was whether she could use them effectively enough to reach the finish line. And beyond that, a nagging thought: what would it take to *change* the rules entirely?

The strategist, Sarah Chen, hadn't slept properly in weeks. Not because of anxiety—she'd run dozens of campaigns, seen far worse late-game scrambles—but from the sheer exhaustion of relentless data analysis. She was staring at a heat map of voter sentiment in three key counties, each dot representing an individual likely to swing one way or another. It looked like static, a blizzard of indecision. The positive ad, a polished piece showcasing her candidate's work on local school funding, had barely registered a blip. Engagement metrics were flat. Social media shares minimal. It wasn't *bad* advertising; it was simply... ignored.

Then she scrolled to the projections for the negative spot—the one highlighting Councilman Davies' vote against a crucial infrastructure bill, couched in language emphasizing potential safety risks to local schools. The data there was unsettlingly clear. A measurable spike in intent to vote for her candidate among those same undecided voters. Not a landslide shift, but enough. Enough to potentially tip the scales.

Sarah remembered her grandfather, a carpenter who'd built houses with his hands before retiring. He used to say that sometimes you had to point out the rot in the wood before people understood the need for repair. It wasn't about being negative; it was about honesty. About acknowledging reality. But that felt like justification, a convenient rationalization. She thought of her daughter, Maya, eight years old and already picking up on the venomous rhetoric filling the airwaves. Maya had asked her just last week why "the nice man" in one ad looked so angry. Sarah hadn't had a good answer.

It wasn't that she enjoyed this part of the job. Quite the opposite. The endless focus-grouping, the meticulous crafting of attack lines, the constant calculating of what would *sting* just enough to motivate a voter without crossing into outright falsehood—it felt... corrosive. Like slowly poisoning the well. But it worked. And in politics, particularly at this level, working mattered. It wasn't about convincing people her candidate was perfect; it was about making them believe the opponent was less fit to serve. A lower bar, certainly, but a bar that seemed stubbornly resistant to being raised.

She thought of the Johnson ad—the little girl and the daisy dissolving into mushroom clouds. The sheer audacity of it. It hadn't argued policy; it had bypassed reason altogether, going straight for the gut. And it had worked, undeniably so. Not because voters were inherently cynical or easily manipulated, but because fear was a more powerful motivator than hope. A threat demanded immediate attention. An opportunity could be deferred. This wasn't about some inherent flaw in the electorate; it was a deeply ingrained survival mechanism playing out on the political stage.

Sarah clicked through a series of case studies—campaigns that had tried, and failed, to run entirely on positive messaging. The data always told the same story: lost ground. Wasted resources. A noble effort, perhaps, but ultimately self-defeating. She remembered one particularly brutal race in Ohio, where a candidate had vowed to remain above the fray, refusing to engage with negative attacks leveled against him. He'd been painted as weak, indecisive—out of touch. The result? A landslide victory for his opponent, who hadn't hesitated to exploit every perceived vulnerability.

It wasn't about being immoral; it was about accepting a fundamental asymmetry in how voters processed information. It felt less like a choice and more like an inevitability. Like gravity. You could try to defy it, but you'd only end up falling harder. But there were degrees of freedom within that constraint. An attack had to be grounded in truth, however selectively presented. It couldn't be pure fabrication. And it had to be proportionate—a response to a genuine threat, not an exaggerated caricature.

She thought about her own mother, a retired librarian who'd dedicated her life to preserving knowledge and fostering critical thinking. Her mother would be horrified by this entire process. She'd see it as a betrayal of everything she stood for. Sarah knew that, and it stung. But she also knew her mother underestimated the sheer noise of modern life—the constant barrage of information, the shrinking attention spans, the relentless competition for eyeballs. In that environment, nuance was a liability. Complexity was ignored. Only the starkest contrasts cut through the clutter.

Sarah rubbed her eyes, feeling the weight of it all pressing down on her. She pulled up an email from Mark Jenkins, a local journalist who'd been covering the race closely. He'd sent a link to an article detailing Davies' recent campaign event—a town hall meeting where he'd dodged questions about the infrastructure bill, offering vague platitudes instead of concrete answers. It was damning evidence, easily verifiable. And it gave her something she hadn't had before: a clear, defensible line of attack.

She started drafting copy for the negative spot, meticulously crafting each sentence to maximize impact while minimizing distortion. She wasn't proud of what she was doing, but she understood it. It wasn't about manipulating voters; it was about competing in a system that rewarded negativity and punished restraint. A system that, frankly, felt broken.

The strategist paused. Was this just accepting the unacceptable? Was there no way to disrupt this cycle of attack ads and distorted truths? She thought back to Eleanor's email—"Beyond the Battlefield." It was more than just a clever phrase; it was a challenge. A call to imagine something different. Something better. But imagining wasn't enough. You had to build it. And building it required winning, first.

Sarah looked at the heat map again. The red dots still flickered with uncertainty. She knew she couldn't change everything overnight. But maybe, just maybe, if her candidate won, they could create a space for a more honest, more constructive kind of politics—a politics based on solutions rather than fear. A politics that appealed to people's better instincts instead of their basest anxieties. It was a long shot, she knew. But it was worth fighting for.

She saved the draft and leaned back in her chair, staring out the window at the gray November sky. The election was just days away. And whatever happened, she suspected this wasn't a battle that would be won or lost on any single campaign ad. It was a deeper struggle—a fight to reclaim the narrative, to redefine what it meant to lead, and to remember, amidst all the noise and fury, why they were even fighting in the first place. The question now wasn't just about winning this election; it was about whether there was enough willingness, on both sides of the aisle, to start building a different kind of battlefield altogether. A space where facts mattered more than fear, and where hope wasn't considered a weakness.

Carol Jensen put down her coffee and walked out. The ad would run another dozen times before Tuesday. She'd probably see most of them. And she'd remember every accusation, word-for-word, long after she'd forgotten what the candidate promised to do.

Carol wanted better news and couldn't look away from the worst. Attack ads work because the asymmetry works, because the thing we say we want loses to the thing we can't stop watching. Which means the question isn't whether we can want our way out. It's whether we can measure our way through.

Chapter 9: Correcting the Scale

You can't unfeel what you just read. The dented rice cooker, the one infection that killed a program that saved thousands, the single sentence that sealed a death sentence — they're in there now, taking up more room than they should. The question isn't whether negativity bias is real. You've already proven it to yourself eight chapters running. The question is what you do when you catch yourself doing it.

Gottman's five-to-one ratio wasn't a suggestion. It was the measured price of overcoming the weight of a single negative interaction. The hospital board needed the same ratio — five recovery stories emphasized for every complication mentioned — and nobody had structured the presentation to give it to them.

The director of quality sat in the front row, taking notes. She'd championed the program. She knew the numbers cold. When the chief medical officer asked his third consecutive question about the single complication—a post-surgical infection in one patient out of four hundred and twelve—she leaned forward to answer, and I could see her doing the mental math in real time, trying to calculate whether this one incident now outweighed two years of work that had cut average recovery time by thirty percent and readmission rates by nearly half.

She was losing that calculation. Not because the math was hard. Because the room had already decided what mattered.

Twenty minutes of relentlessly positive evidence had left almost no impression compared to two minutes describing one thing that went wrong. The CFO had stopped taking notes somewhere around minute twelve of the outcomes presentation. I remember that specifically because I'd been watching him, trying to gauge whether the cost savings were landing. They weren't. But two minutes into the adverse event discussion his pen was back out, underlining something in his printed packet hard enough I could see the indent from across the table. The positive material had been background music. The negative material was the only data point in the room that felt like actual news.

That's what this costs us.

Not abstract epistemic error. Real programs that work, shelved. Real relationships that could recover, abandoned. Real investments that would compound, sold at the bottom because one earnings report felt heavier than three years of growth. We've built an entire cognitive infrastructure around the premise that bad news deserves not just attention but *total override authority*, and we've gotten so practiced at granting it that authority that most of us don't even notice we're doing it anymore.

We just wake up one morning and realize we've been mentally prosecuting our partner for three days over a single offhand comment while a month of daily kindness sits unexamined in the background. Or we've held a stock through five quarters of solid execution and then dumped it forty-eight hours after one disappointing quarter because the recent news somehow felt like the only news that counted. Or we've written off an entire employee based on a performance review that documented one significant mistake and eleven months of reliable work, and when pressed we genuinely can't recall much about those eleven months because the mistake is still taking up most of the available space in memory.

The director of quality left that hospital three months later. Took a position at a competing system across town. I ran into her maybe a year after that at a conference, and she told me the program we'd presented—the one that got shelved after twenty minutes of evidence couldn't outweigh two minutes of concern—had since been quietly restarted at her new hospital, where it was running exactly as designed and producing exactly the outcomes we'd documented. Same protocol. Same results. Different room. She didn't sound triumphant when she told me this. She sounded tired.

And I understood why. Because it meant the problem wasn't the program. It wasn't even the data. The problem was that we'd walked into a room full of intelligent, well-meaning professionals whose entire decision-making apparatus had been calibrated to treat any vivid negative signal as automatically more diagnostic than a mountain of positive evidence, and no amount of preparation or better slides or clearer explanations was going to override that calibration in the moment. The negativity bias wasn't a preference they held. It was the operating system they were running on, and we'd shown up with data formatted for a different OS entirely.

If you've made it this far in this book, you've already felt some version of that cost. You've seen it in the marriage that turned cold because we can't stop mentally replaying the arguments. In the market position we exited too early because the negative headline obliterated our capacity to remember why we bought in the first place. In the jury verdict that turned on aggravating evidence presented for six minutes while mitigating evidence presented for an hour barely moved the needle. The pattern is everywhere.

The question this chapter has to answer is what, exactly, we're supposed to do about it.

And here's where we need to be honest about something most debiasing advice skips right over: the negativity bias isn't a malfunction. It's not some bug in the code we can patch out by sheer force of will or a well-timed reminder to "stay positive." It evolved because it solved a real problem in the ancestral environment it was built for, and it still does genuinely useful work today, every time we notice a warning sign, take a real risk seriously, or catch a problem before it metastasizes. A mind that felt no extra pull toward negative information wouldn't be unbiased. It would be missing a crucial signal. You'd walk into genuinely dangerous situations with the same level of concern you bring to a sunny afternoon, and that would get you hurt.

Daniel Kahneman was once asked after a lecture cataloguing the many ways human judgment reliably misfires whether the goal was to strip out the fast, emotionally weighted responses that produce all these documented errors. Make us think like calculators. His answer was no, and it's worth sitting with why. The goal isn't eliminating the mechanism. It's correcting for the systematic overcorrection in contexts that don't warrant the full-strength ancestral response but trigger it anyway.

A browser tab. A performance review. A headline. A marriage. A stock position. A drug label. A jury room. A campaign ad.

None of these carry anything close to the survival stakes the underlying machinery was calibrated for—the genuinely life-threatening situations where overweighting negative information kept our ancestors alive long enough to become our ancestors—but all of them receive close to the full-strength reaction anyway. That's the gap this chapter is trying to close. Not by asking anyone to feel less alarmed in the moment, which the research suggests is mostly outside our direct control, but by intervening at the one stage that's still open to deliberate correction: the point where a felt reaction gets translated into an actual verdict.

That distinction matters, so let me state it plainly before we turn to technique. The amplification happens automatically. The attention capture, the memory encoding, the way a single negative data point lights up the brain's threat-detection systems like a dashboard warning light—none of that is something we can just decide not to feel. But the gap between feeling that amplification and rendering a final judgment based on it? That gap is where we still have room to work.

The simplest version of that work is a question you ask before committing to a conclusion: *Is this judgment proportional to the full record, or only to the subset my attention naturally prioritized?* The question sounds almost too plain to matter, but its effect is structural. It introduces a mandatory pause between the initial signal—which, again, will skew negative by default—and the final output. That pause doesn't erase the bias. It doesn't make the negative event feel less vivid or the positive ones suddenly flood back into view. What it does is force the rendering process to consult a broader dataset than the one your alarm system handed you.

In practice, that often means building an explicit counter-ledger. If you notice yourself concluding that someone is unreliable because they missed a deadline, the corrective move isn't to talk yourself out of the frustration or pretend the miss didn't happen. It's to ask whether you've recently updated your internal file with the seventeen times they delivered early, the project they salvaged when you were underwater, the standing offer to cover your gaps without being asked. Those entries don't automatically surface during a moment of irritation, so you surface them manually—not to override the negative data, but to restore it to scale.

The same principle applies inward. When the reflex is to treat a mistake as evidence of a deeper inadequacy, the corrective isn't affirmation. It's inventory.

Also in the Series

Every book in The Bias Files stands on its own — read them in any order. If this one was useful, the library continues:

Blind Trust

Can't Let Go

The Planted Price

Why We Fear the Wrong Things

The Expert Trap

Blinded by Brilliance

Cutting Losses

I Knew It All Along

Why Smart People Do Stupid Things

Buying the Top

When Everyone's Buying, Sell

The Invisible Failures

Why It's Never Your Fault

Twice as Long

Words Are Weapons

When Everyone Agrees, You're Wrong

It's Not Them, It's You